marilyn monroe

marilyn monroe

Janice Anderson

This edition produced exclusively for

WHSMITH

Photographic acknowledgments

Camera Press, London 17, 30, 31, 38 bottom, 115, 131, 132, 161, 182–183, 185; Frank Driggs Collection, New York 6 right, 12, 14 right, 15, 16 top, 16 bottom, 20, 21, 26, 27 left, 27 right, 40, 41, 44, 50, 51, 54, 58, 63, 67, 76, 78, 79, 96, 97, 98, 109, 112, 120, 121, 128, 133, 134, 136, 137, 138, 143, 153, 156, 158, 164, 165, 168, 169, 173, 174, 176, 179, 181; Flashbacks, London 28 top, 32, 56, 82; Kobal Collection, London 7, 10, 14, left, 18 top, 18 bottom, 22 top, 22 bottom, 23, 24, 25, 28 bottom, 29, 33, 34, 35 top, 35 bottom, 37 top, 37 bottom, 38 top, 39, 42, 43, 45, 46, 47 bottom, 49, 52, 53, 55, 57, 59 left, 59 right, 60, 61, 64, 65, 66, 68, 71, 72, 73, 74, 75, 77, 80, 81, 84, 85, 86, 87, 88, 90, 93, 94, 99, 100, 101, 102, 103, 104, 105, 106, 107, 108, 110, 111, 113, 117, 118, 119, 122, 123, 124–125, 127, 129, 130, 135, 139, 141, 142, 147, 148, 150, 151, 154, 155, 157, 160, 162–163, 166–167, 172, 175, 177, 180, 186; Eve Arnold 171, 178; National Film Archive, London 6 left, 8, 47 top, 62, 69, 70, 83, 89, 126, 140, 149; Popperfoto, London 9, 116, 144, 146; Rex Features, London 13, 19, 36, 48, 91, 145

Front cover:	Eve Arnold
Back cover:	Kobal Collection, London
Title page:	Kobal Collection, London

**This edition produced exclusively for
W H Smith**

Published by
Deans International Publishing
52–54 Southwark Street, London SE1 1UA
A division of The Hamlyn Publishing Group Limited
London · New York · Sydney · Toronto
Astronaut House, Feltham, Middlesex, England

Printed in Italy

Contents

From Norma Jean to Marilyn

Marilyn Monroe was one of the superstars of the cinema. At the height of her career Alfred Hitchcock said that in his opinion there were then only three genuine female stars in the whole movie industry: Elizabeth Taylor, Ingrid Bergman – and Marilyn. In the mythology of Hollywood she is very, very special. No minor goddess of the pantheon, she is the tops, Aphrodite herself.

The myth of Marilyn Monroe, encouraged undoubtedly by her own belief in the importance of the right publicity to further a girl's career, grew out of her genuinely extraordinarily paradoxical nature.

The milk-and-roses face and the little-girl whispery cooing voice could project a waif-like innocence and the fragility of wind-blown leaves in autumn. In contrast, the gorgeous hour-glass figure projected a voluptuous sexuality. One sensed in her a great physical vitality; the life-force that motivates all great artists, whether actor, musician, painter, sculptor or dancer, and which makes the world reach out for a share of it, was very strong in her.

It was not only her physical nature that was paradoxical; so too was her mental and emotional make-up, which was a mixture of hard-headed determination to succeed and a vulnerable, egotistical need to be loved, to be cared for and to be the pole-star of the lives of those close to her.

Her story has been told many times in many forms, and no doubt will be told many times again. It is our way of having a share of her, of catching at her evanescent life-force so that it is not lost to us forever.

Right: *The Method actress at work. Marilyn, after her stint in the Actors' Studio, New York, returned to Hollywood to play the role of 'chantoose' Cherie in* Bus Stop *(1956).*

Far right: *Top to toe curvaceous glamour in a publicity shot for Twentieth Century-Fox's big budget 1954 musical,* There's No Business Like Show Business.

Opposite: *The invitation in the smouldering eyes gazing from under preposterously lashed lids, the parted lips, the bare shoulders rising out of the expensive fur, and the halo of blonde hair add up to an archetypal Monroe glamour pose.*

Clark Gable and platinum blonde Jean Harlow made a very sexy couple in the 1932 film, Red Dust.

Marilyn Monroe was not her real name, of course. That came much later. It was dreamed up as more suitable for the film star she had always intended to become, from the time as a well-developed teenager she first began to think seriously about making it in the movies.

Her real name was Norma Jean Baker, or perhaps Norma Jean Mortenson; she was never sure who her father was, for she was illegitimate and her mother's clouded mind would not be able to provide an indisputable answer. At least her mother's choice of her daughter's names seemed a nudge in the right direction for someone who might later hope for a movie career, for Norma was also the Christian name of that superstar of the silent screen, Norma Talmadge, who was at the height of her career in the mid-1920s, while Jean was the name of the most sensationally sexy movie star of the 1930s, Jean Harlow.

Her place of birth, too, could hardly have been better for a hopeful film actress, for she was born practically on Hollywood's doorstep in the Los Angeles General Hospital on 1 June 1926. This year was to prove of some significance in the history of the cinema, for Warner Brothers had just acquired a device called Vitaphone that enabled sound on a wax recording to be reproduced in synchronization with a film projector. In December 1926 their first experimental Vitaphone film, *Don Juan*, starring John Barrymore and with a musical score to accompany the silent film, was successfully released. The 'Talkies' were on their way.

The Hollywood of the 1920s had long since lost its quiet, oranges-growing-in-the-desert image, and was the super-elegant, wondrously glamorous home of men and women who were not just 'actors and actresses', but on a par with gods and goddesses, idols to be worshipped as if they existed on some sort of astral plane far removed from the everyday life of ordinary folk.

Many of the stars making films in 1926 can still arouse in us an echo of the wonder, envy and admiration felt by the film-goers of nearly sixty years ago. Among the luminaries of that time were Douglas Fairbanks, Mary Pickford, John Barrymore, Gloria Swanson, Charles Chaplin, Ronald Colman, Joan Crawford, Buster Keaton, Myrna Loy, Ramon Novarro, Lillian Gish and two newcomers Greta Garbo and W.C. Fields (the contrast in styles between the last two is something to savour – no one could say Hollywood cast all its players from the same mould). When the great screen lover Rudolph Valentino died a few weeks after Norma Jean Mortenson was born, his funeral cortège brought New York to a standstill, and thousands of people gathered to watch the passing of his funeral train across America to Los Angeles. It was not just idle curiosity; the watchers, especially the women, felt that they knew Valentino as intimately as if he were a close relative – or a lover.

Norma Jean's mother, Gladys Pearl Baker (née Monroe), worked on the outer fringes of this glamorous world as a film cutter and technician with various companies, including Columbia and R.K.O. Most of her friends were also connected with the film industry, and no doubt they all thought themselves to be, not on the fringes, but an essential part of it. No doubt, too, Gladys and her fellow-workers discussed the lives of their favourite film stars as they sat cutting and splicing reels of film, dreaming rose-coloured dreams about the chances of baby Norma Jean reaching the top in the movie world. Later, Gladys and her good friend Grace McKee took the little girl to Grauman's Chinese Theater to catch something of the aura of all the great stars who had left their signatures and their feet or hand prints in the pavement concrete. At other times they would stand outside picture palaces and hotels where the stars congregated – just a glimpse of someone famous would fuel their dreams and ambitions for weeks ahead.

The world of the movies became, quite naturally, part of Norma Jean's childhood background. There may also have been a more intimate reason for Gladys to think that it was in her daughter's blood, for Gladys Baker was known to have had an affair with a man who worked in the same film company, Consolidated Film Industries, as she did, and who was certainly still around when Gladys became pregnant. He never admitted the connection, however, and showed no further interest in Gladys or her daughter, so maybe Gladys had been right to settle for Edward Mortenson, with whom she had been living, as the father's name to go on her daughter's birth certificate. She could hardly put down her former husband's name, for Mr. Baker, whom she had married in her teens, had left her and divorced her, taking their two children into his care, many months before.

Not that Norwegian-born Edward Mortenson would have anything to do with Norma Jean and her mother either, for he was clearly of a gipsyish disposition, and wandered away from Los Angeles just as he had wandered off and abandoned his family in Norway to come to America. He is thought to have been killed in 1929 when his motorcycle crashed into a car, although another report has him not dying until 1981. If he was Norma Jean's real father, she could have inherited her fair skin, blue-grey eyes and light brown hair from him, although both her red-haired mother and grandmother were said to be very good-looking women.

Looks were not the only thing Norma Jean inherited from her mother's family, though, for there was also a frighteningly large history of insanity. Her maternal grandparents, he of Scottish and she of Irish descent, both apparently suffered from periods of, if not actual insanity, then certainly a lack of balance that

showed itself in terrible rages. Years later, Marilyn used to tell people that she could remember an incident in her babyhood when her grandmother, Della Monroe Grainger, tried to suffocate her. Since Della died in an asylum when Norma Jean was not quite fifteen months old, it seems unlikely that she could 'remember' such an incident, which her then foster parents, the Bolenders, were never heard to mention. On the other hand, the foster parents were clearly frightened of Della and her mad rages, during one of which she tried to batter down the door of their house to get at her granddaughter. They called the police and Della was taken off to the asylum, where she died not very long afterwards.

Gladys Baker herself was to spend much of her adult life in a series of institutions for the mentally ill. Her brother Marion, Norma Jean's uncle, also became insane.

It was a desperately unstable background for the baby to grow up against. Because Gladys, with no man to help her, had to go out to work to support herself and the baby, a foster home had to be found for Norma Jean. Ida and Wayne Bolender, quiet, good-living and honest folk, were the first of a series of foster

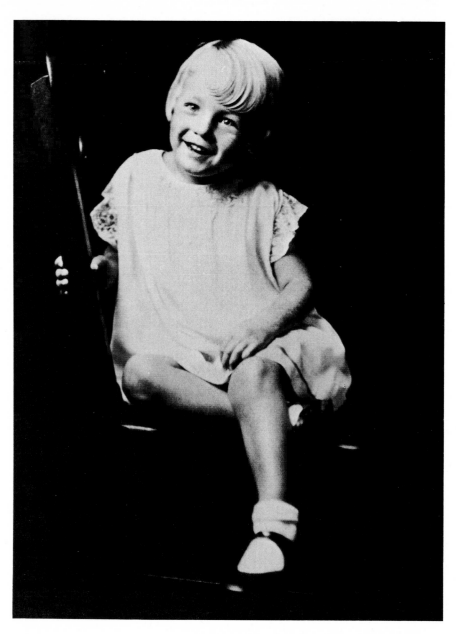

Before life got complicated: a happy, smiling Norma Jean aged about six.

understand the difference and to see it as the Bolenders expressing a greater love for Lester than for herself. It is possible the Bolenders could not afford to adopt both children, and thus lose two sets of fostering payments. (But still, Norma Jean would think, they chose Lester, not me.) For the reason for the Bolender's decision it is probably more realistic to look at Gladys Baker's attitude to her child. From the outset she had shown a strong determination to keep the child and to try to make a home for her, and it was for that reason that she was working to save money so that she could find a place for the two of them. Arranging for her child to be fostered was one thing; at least it ensured Norma Jean a good roof over her head and proper care and attention. But to have her adopted was quite unacceptable; that would be to give her away for ever.

Eventually, Gladys saved enough money to be able to buy a house of her own in Hollywood. To help pay the instalments on it, she let off part of it to an English couple who worked as extras in various films. Then she took Norma Jean away from the Bolenders and brought her to the house in Hollywood.

The scheme, nurtured by Gladys Baker for seven years, did not work out. Within three months she had suffered a complete nervous breakdown. One day Norma Jean came home from school to be told that her mother was very sick and had been taken to hospital; she would be nearly 20 before she would live with her mother again, or find out just what was wrong with her. In the meantime, the English couple did their casual best to look after Norma Jean, though she must have found them a rather alarming substitute for the Bolenders, what with their smoking and drinking, their much more sophisticated behaviour and their alien, English accents.

When they returned to England, and a neighbour's tentative efforts to adopt Norma Jean came to nothing, there was nowhere else for the child to go but to an orphanage. She was found a place in the Los Angeles Orphans' Home by her mother's old friend, Grace McKee, who was made her legal guardian after Gladys had been taken to the asylum – the same institution, distressingly enough, in which Della had died.

parents in the girl's childhood. They were also the longest-lasting, for Norma Jean spent the first seven years of her life with them. It was not long before the little girl was as confused about who her real mother was as she was about her father. One reason for this was that the Bolenders lived a long tram ride out of Los Angeles and so Gladys could only get to see her daughter at weekends, and sometimes not every weekend.

The Bolenders were able to give their foster daughter a pretty normal and even comfortable life. She was well cared for, well fed and clothed, and given piano lessons. There was even a foster brother, Lester, to play with. Judging by their photographs, the two children were an attractively healthy and bonny pair.

The Bolenders adopted Lester, but not Norma Jean. The girl was old enough to

It is clear that the walk over the threshold of the children's home with the word 'Orphan' at the entrance for all to see was one of the major traumatic events of Norma Jean Mortenson's young life. The shock to the nine-year-old child was stunning. She was not an orphan: she had a mother, so how could she be an orphan? Yet 'Aunt' Grace was putting her into an orphanage, abandoning her.

The arrival at the orphanage door marks the beginning, the first act in the creation of the myth of Marilyn Monroe – surely the most potent myth in the short history of the cinema. It was a myth that Marilyn Monroe created for her film-star persona out of the loveless and soul-destroying greyness of her life in the orphanage. It was not that they mistreated her; indeed, they did their best to make her feel loved and wanted. But she hated it, withdrawing more and more into the private world of her own mind.

Norma Jean spent nearly two years in the Los Angeles orphanage, after which there were more foster homes. She must have become totally confused about what life and the world expected of her as she went from one foster home and its set of attitudes and values to another. Perhaps, too, at war with this confusion in her mind was the thought that the world did not expect anything of her at all, for the world had decided she was of no importance – just a piece of human flotsam to be washed about from one empty shore to another. Out of such thoughts grew her determination to be someone, to be a personality whose importance would be recognized by the whole world. If nobody else believed in her, then she, Norma Jean, would believe in herself so much that everyone would be forced to take notice, to accept her world her way.

Later, when Marilyn Monroe would recount the story of her childhood, it all had to be dramatized, made into something larger, more colourful than drab reality.

Her mother had abandoned Norma Jean, so Marilyn Monroe would have no mother. Grace McKee had put Norma Jean in the orphanage, so Grace McKee who in reality cared deeply for her, visiting her every week at the orphanage, taking her out, giving her presents, finally taking her into her own home, was given

little part and no love in the Monroe mythology.

Gradually, the myth was embellished. When young Jim Dougherty married Norma Jean shortly after her sixteenth birthday, he married a virgin, or so he has maintained ever since. But Marilyn Monroe's childhood, besides including more foster homes than Norma Jean knew in reality, included one in which the child was raped when she was about eight by a man who rented a room in the house.

By the time she left the orphanage, aged eleven, Norma Jean was already noticing herself; already, with Grace McKee's help, experimenting with lipstick and hair curlers, even a little powder on her nose. She may even have seen that her rather lumpy nose was not her best feature, but soon this minor defect was more than cancelled out by the effect she created when she took to wearing sweaters on her well-developed body. The boys certainly noticed Norma Jean then.

There would seem to have been two more foster homes for Norma Jean to cope with before she finally went to live with Grace McKee and her new husband, Erwin Goddard, an engineer with children of his own. Their home was in Van Nuys, just north of Hollywood and Beverly Hills. Norma Jean's destiny was gravitating back towards movie-land, but first, the teenage Norma Jean had to get through high school and grow up a little more.

She was an undistinguished student at both the schools she attended in Van Nuys. She was not too bad in her English classes, however – she would later read and write poetry with some dedication – and appears to have made a vague attempt at acting, but the Van Nuys High School Dramatic Society saw no potential in her and she was not given any parts in their productions. Whatever she came to know about acting was certainly not 'learned' at school. In fact, Norma Jean was a very quiet girl, keeping herself to herself. At least, so it would appear, until she wore a sweater. Then she would make the High School boys think some very unquiet thoughts: the later extraordinary duality of her personality was already in evidence.

It was while living with Grace McKee Goddard that Norma Jean came to know the one person for whom she felt any real affection during her childhood. This was Grace's aunt, Ana Lower, a Christian Scientist for whose sake Norma Jean started going to church regularly on Sunday. When she was about fifteen, she lived for a year with 'Aunt' Ana.

By this time, Norma Jean, already physically well-developed, had reached puberty. Boys were attracted to her like bees to a honey-pot, and she was always out on a date or on the beach with some smart boy or other – or so it seemed to Aunts Grace and Ana. They were worried, and with reason, for Norma Jean seemed coolly innocent in sexual matters and quite unaware that the effect she had on boys was a highly sexual once. The aunts could foresee problems ahead. For one thing, Ana Lower was now too old and sick to be able to make a home for Norma Jean, and for another, Grace Goddard and her family were planning to move across country to a new job for Erwin Goddard. As they talked round and round the problem of what should be done with their charge that would not involve the orphanage or a foster home again, a solution emerged – marriage. They even had nineteen-year-old Jim Dougherty in mind, son of friends of the Goddards.

The fresh and uncomplicated all-American outdoor girl, as personified by photographers' model Norma Jean Dougherty, 1946–7.

Manoeuvred into a date with Norma Jean, Jim soon found himself sufficiently attracted to take her out again, and again. Within months they were engaged and in June 1942, they were married. Norma Jean, wearing a long white dress and veil made by Aunt Ana, and burdened with a large bouquet of white flowers, looks sweet, tender and very young on the wedding photographs. Jim looks like what he was – a pleasant, likeable lad.

The marriage was not a bad one as marriages go. Jim had a job, Norma Jean did the housework and learned to cook – after a fashion – and the young couple saw quite a lot of his family. Then the Second World War caught up with them and in 1944 Jim enlisted in the U.S. Merchant Marine as a physical training instructor. Norma Jean joined him at the base where he was stationed – and soon found herself surrounded by men much more appreciative of her splendid physical attributes than Jim appeared to be. Suddenly, the horizon of her world, for the past two years reduced to that of a rather bored and certainly suppressed housewife, widened appreciably.

She began wearing tight clothes again and swinging her hips when she walked. The men stared and whistled – and Jim hated it. He remonstrated with her, and when she whispered in his ear of her ambition to make it in the movies, he told her that she should forget such nonsense, there were already hundreds of prettier girls than her haunting Hollywood and, anyway, she was his wife. It sounded as if he meant 'his property'. Perhaps he did, for Jim was an old-fashioned, unimaginative man; the salt of the earth, no doubt, but ill-equipped to deal with a woman like Norma Jean.

All too soon, Jim was deprived of his land-based instructor's job and sent to sea. Although his wife moved in with his parents and their family, it was not enough to keep Norma Jean mentally in tune with her husband. Their physical separation quickly became for her a total separation. She was on her own, able to do her own thing.

Her first move was reasonable enough; she found herself a job. Her contribution to America's war effort was to inspect parachutes at the Radio Planes Parts Company in Burbank where her mother-

in-law was working. From all accounts Norma worked hard, and after a while she was moved to the 'dope room' where she sprayed fuselage parts. The job involved wearing overalls, and Norma Jean knew instinctively how to wear overalls to good effect. In fact, they helped give her contribution to the war effort a whole new dimension, for one day she was spotted at work by an Army photographer, David Conover, sent to the factory to get some good pictures of women at work for *Yank* magazine. He thought Norma Jean looked pretty good at work, photographed her and discovered in the pictures that came out of his camera a girl whose natural good looks and glowing vitality were magnified and enhanced many times over by the lens. Black-and-white or colour, in over-

Norma Jean's modelling career was only just beginning when this pose was struck.

Right: *Charming and natural, but not yet very sophisticated, could be the verdict on this early modelling shot, c. 1947.*

Far right: *No bean-pole thin fashion magazine model, the well-endowed Norma Jean goes for the exuberant, wind-swept look in this modelling shot from 1946–7.*

Opposite: *That striped two-piece with the strategically-placed knotted ties turns up again in this 1946–7 pin-up, and Norma Jean looks pretty enticing in it as she kneels on the end of a swimming pool diving board.*

She worked hard at being a model, taking her classes seriously, trying to learn from the mistakes that produced the inevitable bad pictures that came out of photographic sessions. It was now, not later when she was a big star with an image to protect, that she developed the habit of studying carefully all the prints from photographic sessions. It was a serious profession she was entering and she took to it with professional dedication.

At Miss Snively's insistence Norma Jean also, reluctantly, became a blonde. She did not want to, for her it was not 'real', and surely it did not matter all that much? Miss Snively assured her it did, saying that her sun-lightened hair looked dark and dull on photographs, and that she would not get good jobs unless it were lighter. Norma Jean Mortenson was beginning to lose her identity, her image

alls or sweater, the effect was the same: Norma Jean Dougherty caught and held the attention of every man who saw the prints.

One of the men who saw them was a commercial photographer called Potter Hueth who was impressed enough to arrange a few photographic sessions with Norma Jean after work. He could not afford to pay her in hard cash, so instead showed her photographs to Miss Emmeline Snively of the Blue Book Model Agency in Hollywood, and got her an appointment. Miss Snively took her on.

It was June 1945, and Norma Jean's foot (which she was to discover exactly fitted Valentino's print outside Grauman's Chinese Theater: another omen?) was inside Hollywood's door, for everyone knew that being a successful model was as sure a road as any in that town where nothing was sure, towards getting into the movies. It was at least as sure as sitting around on a soda-fountain stool waiting to be noticed, à la Lana Turner, and Norma Jean was not one for sitting around.

15

Below: *Still in pursuit of the outdoors image, Norma Jean takes up a bow and arrow for this pose from her mid-1940s modelling period.*

was losing out to that of the film star she was to become.

Not that this worried her at the time – far from it – she was exultant, optimistic. Life was looking up. She left the job with the aircraft factory and moved back with Aunt Ana, which was where Jim found her when he came home on leave.

Jim also met Gladys Baker for the first time. She was out of the mental institution that had been her home for nearly twelve years, and for a time tried to make another home for herself with Norma Jean. She was still far from normal mentally, and a long way from being cured. Worry about her daughter probably increased her depression. Norma Jean's marriage was clearly over: not only did she file for a divorce but she also left her mother to go away on a month-long photographic trip with photographer André de Dienes, during the course of which they became lovers. It was probably her first infidelity and a sign that she regarded her marriage as finished. Then, understandably perhaps, there seems to have been little intimacy between mother and daughter – no coming together of minds or emotions. So, after seven months of sharing an apartment with Norma Jean, Gladys asked to go back to the mental home.

By October 1946, with her mother back in the institution and her husband divorced in Reno, Norma Jean was on the brink of a blossoming modelling career, of which André de Dienes's lovely photographs taken on their trip through the American West are the finest reminders.

They show a young woman in the first flush of adult beauty. There is still something of the virginal girl in the rounded, shiny face and the uncomplicated, ingenuous smile, bright red lips stretched wide to show perfect teeth. The eyes, gazing at the camera, look innocent, without guile. The wavy hair, still fair rather than blonde, is simply brushed back from the broad, unlined brow. It is the face of a clean, wholesome American girl. The body, however, is quite another matter! The hips have a sexy, even arrogant tilt, emphasized by the hands casually, carelessly pulling down the jeans' belt carriers so that a tantalizing section of white body can be glimpsed between the jeans and the blouse, knotted under the gently curving breasts.

Another portrait from the series taken by André de Dienes in California in 1945.

No wonder André de Dienes was in love with her by the time they got back to Los Angeles. They even talked of marriage, though she was not yet divorced. It came to nothing of course. Norma Jean was too engrossed in her as yet unfulfilled ambitions to think of getting married again. Still, de Dienes's photographs of her appeared on the covers of several big-selling American magazines, which did neither of them any harm.

Her photograph was appearing with increasing frequency on American newsstands. It was even rumoured, and the rumour was printed, that millionaire movie magnate Howard Hughes, struggling back to life after an appalling plane crash in July 1946 which had left him with severe multiple injuries, sat up – mentally, if not physically – and started taking notice of the girl on all the cheesecake magazines. Now, Howard Hughes had practically invented the screen career of Miss Jane Russell and her wonderful, notorious cantilevered bosom: had he seen similar potential in the latest cover-girl?

It did not matter whether he had or not. It was as good a pretext as any for an agent looking for an opening for his client. Miss Snively had got Norma Jean a genuine

Right: *Norma Jean posing for Hollywood cameraman Leo Caloia in 1946: a scene from the film* Hollywood . . . History or Hysterics.

Below: *Monroe learning her trade – another mid-40s pose.*

Hollywood agent, and he approached Ben Lyon, former film actor and now casting director at Twentieth Century-Fox, for an interview. To his credit, Lyon saw the potential in the shy, inexperienced model who came to his office, and arranged for her to be screen-tested on the set of a film called *Mother Wore Tights*, starring Fox's resident blonde bombshell and Number One Pin-Up Betty Grable.

The test looked good, for Norma Jean on celluloid had what the cameramen called 'flesh impact'. Even Fox dictator Darryl F. Zanuck was impressed enough to agree that the girl should be put under contract. It did not mean all that much to him, he had dozens of good-looking girls under contract, most of whom would never amount to anything, but it meant the whole world to her.

Ben Lyon did not like her name. Norma Jean Dougherty was much too inelegant for a movie star. He suggested Marilyn might be a good first name (he had once been engaged to a musical comedy star called – the ironies of Hollywood! – Marilyn Miller), and left her to think up a surname to go with it. Aunt Grace Goddard, still her legal guardian, was called on by an excited Norma Jean to countersign the contract. Aunt Grace, just as excited, did, then suggested 'Monroe', Gladys's maiden name, to go with 'Marilyn'. It sounded good; there had even been a President of the United States called Monroe. So Marilyn Monroe it was, as from August 1946.

A Hollywood starlet emerging. Photographer Bernard of Hollywood took this picture of sweatergirl Marilyn Monroe in 1948 as part of her campaign to get herself noticed in the Hollywood jungle.

Genesis of a Hollywood Blonde

Opposite: *One of the earliest publicity stills taken of Marilyn Monroe, movie starlet; this picture of sweet, ruffle-bloused innocence dates from 1948.*

Blink, and you would miss Marilyn Monroe's background role in the first film she made. This was *Scudda-Hoo! Scudda-Hay!*, released in March 1948 and later re-titled *Summer Lightning*. She had been under contract to Twentieth Century-Fox for several months when she was eventually told she had a part in a film. Perhaps she thought it was going to be her first big step up the ladder. In fact, she was probably just lucky to have been chosen – rather like a name drawn from a hat – for a bit part in this June Haver movie.

Haver herself had been groomed by Fox to take over from Betty Grable as the studio's Number One blonde bombshell, so there is some typically Hollywood irony lurking behind Marilyn's presence among the bit players assembled for the film: it would be Monroe, not Haver, who would eventually take over the vast Grable dressing room on the Fox lot.

Right: Marilyn threw herself with dedication into the business of turning a pretty girl into a movie starlet. Here she practises a dramatic school exercise with other young hopefuls.

Monroe's training for *Scudda-Hoo! Scudda-Hay!* had included singing, dancing, movement and acting lessons in the studio's classes, and a full course of the publicity treatment meted out to all contract employees. This involved appearing in the right restaurants with the right escort when the studio demanded it, waving from carnival floats with the right amount of girlish enthusiasm and beauty, posing for uncounted hours for the stills, pin-up and cheesecake photographs that were all grist to the studio's publicity mill.

She had taken – and would always take – the acting lessons seriously, attending classes at the Actor's Lab where Morris Carnovsky and Phoebe Brand carried on the traditions and beliefs of the Group Theatre of New York, purveyor in the 1930s of a potent mixture of the methods of Stanislavsky and the political beliefs of European left-wingers. Not that Monroe contributed much to her acting classes. She mostly just sat silent in the background. No one noticed any particular ability or talent in her.

She took her personal appearance seriously, too, doing hours of exercise for her figure, even getting up early in the morning to run around the block a few times, perhaps ride a bicycle, certainly exercise with dumb-bells. She must also have spent much time in front of her mirror experimenting with make-up, for she very soon became an expert, discovering all the tricks that could turn a pretty girl into a ravishing beauty.

All in all, it was a girl raring to go who reported for her first day's work on *Scudda-Hoo! Scudda-Hay!* The film was to be in Technicolor, which would surely only enhance her glowing, twenty-one-year-old's good looks. She discovered she had just one line to say – in fact just one

Right: *The exuberant, sexy-blonde look: a sweater and shorts help to show off the Monroe vital statistics in this 1949 pin-up shot.*

Below: *Marilyn enjoyed the obligatory starlet's work of posing for pin-up and publicity stills.*

word, 'Hello' – and that for the most part she would remain with the pack of extras. She did at least get on to film, and there are stills around to prove it, but it all ended up on the cutting-room floor, except for a short section with her and another bit-part actress, Colleen Townsend, in a rowing boat so far in the background, their faces are unrecognizable.

Scudda-Hoo! Scudda-Hay! was directed by F. Hugh Herbert. He was vastly experienced in film-making and with a long string of movies, silent and talking, to his credit, both as script-writer and director; he was to achieve a certain notoriety in the 1950s when the screen version of his play *The Moon is Blue* included the shocking word 'virgin'. Not that there was anything notorious about *Scudda-Hoo! Scudda-Hay!*, however, which turned out to be a mildly amusing tale about a farm boy (Lon McCallister) with a talent for training difficult mules. June Haver came into it as his farm-girl romantic interest. Other stars were Walter Brennan and child star Natalie Wood, who had fifth billing as Bean McGill.

For Monroe, it was a start. At least she now knew what it felt like to be on a film set, under the lights and in front of the cameras, learning who did what, how the various members of the film crew could be vital to a girl's future, who it might be a mistake to ignore, and especially how you could project your personality so that it stood out from the pack.

More experience was gained in *Dangerous Years*, released by Twentieth Century-Fox at the end of 1947. Her screen-time was rather longer in this one – in fact she even got on the cast list, fourteenth out of fifteen named players. She played a slightly brassy, rather over made-up and vulgar waitress in a juke-box joint. Whatever impact she made it certainly wasn't as a potential successor to Betty Grable or June Haver.

Dangerous Years was a melodrama about juvenile delinquency, directed by Arthur Pierson. It was the story of a boy, Danny (William Halop), reared in an orphanage, who became a delinquent, finally killing Jeff Carter (Donald Curtis) who had been running a boy's club that had been instrumental in stopping local kids going to the bad.

The film was made by an independent producer of low-budget movies, Sol Wurtzel, and released through Fox. There was not a lot in it for Monroe to do, and she did not impress anyone. The option on her contract, under which she was now getting $150 a week, a princely sum that had allowed her to buy the first 'good' clothes she had ever owned, was up by this time, and Fox decided they did not want to sign her up. Thus in August 1947, starlet Marilyn Monroe was without a studio or any obvious way of making a living. There were to be several years of hand-to-mouth existence ahead before the girl who had already had plenty of that could see a light at the end of the tunnel. Or perhaps hole would be a better description – the sort of hole Alice fell down, reaching out for things as she tumbled past until she landed, more or less safely, at the bottom outside the door to Wonderland.

Among the things Marilyn reached out for on her way to Hollywood's Wonder-

Some film never made it to the screen: this scene from Scudda Hoo! Scudda Hay! *(1948), in which Marilyn Monroe and Colleen Townsend paddle up for a better view of Robert Karnes, ended up on the cutting room floor.*

Marilyn had a bit part as a waitress in a juke-box joint in Dangerous Years *(1947). Here, she manages an enthusiastic smile for Donald Curtis.*

land of success and star status were modelling jobs that would pay the rent and the cost of her acting lessons – and men who might provide meal tickets. Marilyn had plenty of dates and after a while rumours began to circulate about what she got up to in her private life. The difficulty for the biographer trying to weigh up the pros and cons of Marilyn's behaviour in these lean years lies in her own strangely schizophrenic attitude to sex and men. On the one hand, she seems to have retained certain puritanical and romantic notions about the relationship between men and women. It caused her to reject more than one coarse pass from men who made it clear they thought she should be happy to allow them the use of her gorgeous body in return for a meal, a $50 'cloakroom tip' or the promise of a film

role some time in the unspecified future. In this, she seems to have lacked the hard, business-is-business-is-sex-if-necessary attitude to be found in so many young women on the make in Hollywood.

On the other hand, she seems not to have minded sleeping around with men who might be of immediate help to her, provided she made the choice for herself; no one was going to push Marilyn Monroe around. Maybe too, as her detractors have said, she was too shrewd to play the prostitute, and chose very carefully the men with whom she would have relationships in the furtherance of her career.

Be that as it may, it was not long before she was being seen in close company with Joseph Schenck, co-founder with Darryl Zanuck of the film company Twentieth

Century, which had merged with Fox in 1935. By the time Marilyn came his way he was no longer a great power in the company, though he was still with it as executive producer. Nearly seventy years old, he was also well past his peak as the kind of sexual athlete who had helped make the legend of the Hollywood casting couch; so Marilyn's assertion that they were just good friends may well be the truth, unlikely as it seems. Perhaps she hoped that he still had enough power and contacts to help her career; perhaps she thought she might learn something about the movie jungle from someone who had prowled successfully through it for years, or maybe naïve little Norma Jean just liked having someone other than the girls in her cheap rooming house to talk to.

About six months after Fox dropped Monroe's name from their list of contract players, she was called to Columbia Pictures. It may have been Schenck's influence with Columbia boss Henry Cohen at work, or possibly it was her agent doing his job. He persuaded Max Arnow, head of Columbia's talent-spotting team, to look at the screen test on the set of *Mother Wore Tights*, which had persuaded Zanuck to hire Monroe. Arnow was impressed and Monroe signed a six-month option contract in March 1948.

A 1948 cheesecake pose which allows the Monroe legs to be seen to good effect.

Since Columbia just then had no film on the stocks with any part suitable for Marilyn, they sent her to their acting coach, Natasha Lytess, for lessons. Miss Lytess, once an actress in the company of the hugely influential German stage director Max Reinhardt, was not impressed by what she first saw. Monroe seemed talentless, dim, rather vulgar and without even a good voice. She soon discovered that this apparently typical Hollywood starlet was possessed by a demon to learn and a powerful desire to become a real actress. She was also to learn that Monroe in front of a camera was a transformed creature. Miss Lytess became the first real ally Monroe was to find in Hollywood and a close friend. She taught Marilyn how to speak her lines, how to project her voice, how to evaluate a script. She was, in fact, a corner stone in the building of Marilyn Monroe, actress.

Columbia found a part for their new blonde in a B-grade musical, *Ladies of the Chorus*, in which Monroe had second billing after Adele Jergens, a plantinum blonde stalwart of many B-grade, low-budget films. *Ladies of the Chorus*, an unlikely story of back-stage romance, was made in eleven days using a cast of little-known and little-talented players. Among

other improbabilities, the film called upon its audiences to believe that Miss Jergens, born in 1917, was the mother of Miss Monroe – born in 1926! Miss Jergens may have been a couple of inches taller than the 5ft 5½in. Miss Monroe but she certainly did not look a great deal older. In fact, if the film demonstrated anything, it was that Marilyn was not cut out to be the ideal chorus girl – her lovely, sexy legs were also the shortest in the line.

In *Ladies of the Chorus*, Monroe played Peggy, an innocent good-living young star of burlesque (another improbability?) who falls in love with the son of a rich family, played by the very ordinary Rand Brooks. Her mother, having a failed marriage to a rich young man behind her, is worried; his mother, at first disapproving, decides that Peggy is a fine young lady and puts no obstacle in the way of the marriage. The film ends in wedding bells all round, for Peggy's mother also marries again, this time to Billy, the burlesque show's resident comic, played by Eddie Garr.

Even in this dud picture, Monroe's ability to use the camera to project a character compounded of innocent warmth and startling sex appeal somehow came through. She looked pretty, albeit a

Opposite: *More poolside glamour from a beautiful Californian blonde, c. 1949.*

Left and far left: *Guess the emotions on display: Marilyn being coached in how to express her feelings on screen in a drama school exercise.*

27

Above: *Publicity material for* Ladies of the Chorus *(1948)*.

bit vacant; she acted none too badly, though the inexperience showed; she danced a bit and she sang quite charmingly. At last the world was getting a glimpse of the possibilities of Marilyn Monroe.

She had two songs in the film, 'Every Baby Needs a Da Da Daddy', and 'Anyone Can Tell I Love You', both written by Allan Roberts and Lester Lee. The 'Da Da Daddy' number was sung by Marilyn and a chorus of eight young lovelies, each holding a curly-haired 'Raggedy Ann' doll. The lovelies were all dressed in thigh-high dresses trimmed with frilly net and covered in polka-dots, and with strange silvery net bows on their heads – fine examples of Hollywood kitsch, in fact. Marilyn was allowed to wear a long slinky black dress slit to the thigh to reveal fish-net tights: kitsch, too,

Right: *Adele Jergens and Marilyn Monroe played mother and daughter in* Ladies of the Chorus.

The chorus singing 'Every Baby Needs a Da Da Daddy' and holding dolls to prove it, in Ladies of the Chorus. *Monroe, in black slit-side dress and fishnet tights, has no difficulty in standing out from the rest.*

of course, but very sexy. Her other song was a duet, sung with Rand Brooks.

Marilyn had had hours of coaching from Columbia's musical director, Fred Karger, and if the *Motion Picture Herald* reported that Miss Monroe's singing was 'pleasing', then it is to Karger that most of the credit should go. He spent hours with her, going over her songs note by note, phrase by phrase. Fortunately, her voice, though small, could hold a tune so at least Karger had something to work on.

In the end, Karger also had a relationship to work on. He took Marilyn home to supper; his women folk liked her, she liked them. He found her somewhere better to live than the one-room apartment in which she then lived with her pet dog and 200 books, he took her to concerts, to dinners, out dancing. Recently divorced and with a small son, Karger found that Marilyn filled some sort of void in his life. As for Marilyn, she seems to have fallen considerably in love with Karger, partly for his own sake, and partly, perhaps, for his home life which at that time was centred on his warm, loving, expert cook mother, and his sister. Soon they were having an affair which, on her side at least, was one of the most important events her emotional life had known till then.

It was just as well she had something positive in her life because in September 1948 Columbia, like Twentieth Century-Fox a year before, did not take up their option on her contract. Once again it was no studio, no job – and no romance, for the affair with Karger had ended too (Karger eventually married Jane Wyman not long before Wyman's ex-husband, the actor Ronald Reagan, married starlet Nancy Davis).

With hindsight, and looking at the Marilyn of *Ladies of the Chorus* with the later, perfect Marilyn in mind, it is easy to assume that the executives of Columbia went about with eyes, ears and minds closed. How could they toss aside such a gorgeous girl who created a kind of magic every time she walked in front of the camera? The truth is, of course, that although the potential *was* there if you looked carefully using your imagination, the studio executives did not have to look carefully or imaginatively: they already had plenty of lovely, glamorous girls in stock, so why add another $200-worth a week to the payroll. Then, too, Darryl Zanuck may have passed on to Harry Cohen his opinion of Monroe. Zanuck knew all about those rumours of what Monroe had been up to in the offices of Fox executives in the late afternoons and, talent or no talent, he wanted nothing to do with her again – as Joe Mankiewicz reported years later when recalling how violently opposed Zanuck had been to giving Monroe the part of Miss Caswell in *All About Eve*.

Above: *Monroe's wonderful vitality captured by the camera of André de Dienes at Jones Beach, New York, in 1950.*

Opposite: *The young Marilyn's fresh loveliness caught in a casual, relaxed shot by André de Dienes also taken at Jones Beach.*

as reticence, but as a great loneliness. It was as if the girl from the orphanage had never learned to communicate with others, and would always be alone even in a crowd.

Some of her modelling work at this time was for magazine illustrator Ed Moran, who specialized in the healthy, all-American girl type, but one job, the most famous of her modelling career, was for photographer Tom Kelley.

She had worked with Kelley before, always for advertisements. He had asked her to pose nude for him – the money was good if you had a beautiful body – but she had always refused. Then came the day in 1949 when her need of money, to pay the rent and to get back her car which had been repossessed for non-payment of the hire-purchase instalments, overcame her scruples. She telephoned Kelley, arranged a time and got an assurance that only Kelley and his wife would be in on the session.

She ended up with $50 for her nude modelling. Kelley, on the other hand, got less than $900 for the two pictures that were to become famous and make other people a lot of money indeed.

They appeared in 1952 in the guise of calendars called 'Golden Dreams' and 'A New Wrinkle', of the kind that hung in garage workshops or men's washrooms the world over. They would probably have made no more of an impression than any others of their type were it not for the fact that they appeared at a time when Monroe was being talked about everywhere as a rising star. The consequent furore has given the photographs a kind of immortality: writers have even been known to dub them, presumably referring to their artistic pretensions, as 'Monroe Desnuda', as if Kelley were a latter-day Goya.

He was not, of course, and the photographs would be merely pin-ups were it not for the fact that it is Marilyn Monroe who is revealed naked for all the world to see. The photographs are typical soft-pornography of their time, made acceptable and given a certain respectability by the poses, derived from classical art, in which the model is photographed. In the 1980s, because our eyes are accustomed to the lubricious vulgarity displayed in so many girlie magazines, the photographs

Once again, she found herself taking modelling jobs where she, or her agent, could find them, accepting all the dinner invitations that came her way, carrying on with the acting lessons and just grimly hanging on. Sometimes she had a room in the Studio Club, an inexpensive and respectable haven for aspiring actresses, sometimes she lived in hotels, and sometimes with friends like Natasha Lytess, who commented later that she often found her house guest reticent, uncommunicative and inclined to retire into the world of her own mind. This trait, this impression she often gave of simply not being there when spoken to, was noticed by many people, some of whom saw it not

seem bland – 'What a pretty girl, what a beautiful body,' we think, noting inconsequentially what a lovely colour her hair was in those far-off, innocent times.

Not long after this episode, Marilyn, by her own account, won for herself her next film role. She heard that a sexy blonde was needed over at the R.K.O. lot to complete an independently produced Marx Brothers movie, telephoned the producer and talked herself into an appointment to be viewed.

She must by this time have perfected the Monroe Walk – that extraordinary, inimitable and uniquely sexy invitation she managed to convey with every wiggle of her hips – for she only had to walk across producer Lester Cowan's office in front of Groucho Marx in order to get the job.

The film was *Love Happy*, released by United Artists in 1949 and, although hers was only a walk-on part, Groucho, having seen those hips in action, wrote a line of dialogue for her. Groucho played private detective Sam Grunion hot on the trail of the stolen Romanoff diamonds which villainess Madame Egilichi (Ilona Massey) had smuggled into the U.S. in a can of sardines(!) Following the trail of the sardine can into a theatre, Grunion is accosted by a wondrously shapely blonde who says in her breathless little girl voice that she needs his help because 'men keep following me all the time'. Her exit allows anyone who has not already noticed to see why she has this problem.

And that was it, but it was enough, for it is from *Love Happy* that one can date the first signs of that murmuring of public opinion at first so low the studio bosses could ignore it, which was to become a groundswell, then a mighty tide that swept Monroe to stardom, in spite of, rather than because of, the Hollywood star system.

Opposite: *How to capture the attention of America's pin-up fans – a sexy, suggestive pose* c. 1950.

Below: *Sun, sea and sex: an irresistible combination for a memorable pin-up.*

Making the most of a brief appearance in the Marx Brothers' Love Happy *(1949), Monroe provides a dazzling smile for this still with Groucho.*

Monroe was a little bit lucky, because *Love Happy* was the first film the Marx Brothers had made together since *A Night in Casablanca* just after the War, and the critics noted it, if only to see how the zany twenty-year-old partnership was holding up. It was also, as it happened, the Brothers' last film together.

Lester Cowan was at first full of enthusiasm for his new discovery – who desperately hoped to be given a contract by him – and sent Marilyn east to cross America on a publicity spree for *Love Happy*, which had not yet been released. New York was having a heat wave, and Marilyn found herself being photographed in variations of the theme 'Hollywood's hottest new property cooling off in New York'.

It was her first time in New York and she may well have liked to see what the legitimate theatre was up to, or view a few galleries, or just walk in Central Park. Instead, she got one trip to Jones Beach where admittedly photographer André de Dienes surpassed himself by taking some of the best pictures ever of Marilyn, full of a wonderful exuberance, vitality and female sex-appeal. For the rest, she spent all her time being pushed from one photo-call to another, from one meeting with news reporters or gossip columnists to another. Still, she did get mentions in the gossip columns, her photographs in New York's newspapers, and her voice was heard on radio interviews: clearly she was a film actress who looked to New York as if she was on the way up.

After a few weeks of this sort of thing in the cities of the mid-West, Monroe decided that even if she wanted to keep on going up this wasn't the way to do it. She quit the publicity tour and headed back to Hollywood. No Lester Cowan, no contract, no job – but there was another man.

Waiting to step into her life was Johnny Hyde, one of Hollywood's best agents. He had seen her in *Love Happy*, and had fallen hard, both for the girl herself and for the star potential he saw in her. Soon, Johnny Hyde's William Morris agency had taken her on and he was pushing her star potential everywhere, including some very high-up places in the Hollywood hierarchy, for Johnny Hyde knew and was friendly with many of the most important producers in the film business.

Above: *In another pose for the pin-up market, Marilyn stretches blissfully in the sun on a California beach.*

Left: *'men keep following me all the time,' Marilyn told Groucho Marx in* Love Happy. *'Like this?' Groucho seems to be demonstrating, having taken off his glasses to get closer to the lovely armful.*

Hollywood agent Johnny Hyde, seen here poolside with Marilyn, was a major influence on her early career, providing good advice and obtaining two juicy parts for her.

Soon, too, the rather odd couple of Hyde and Monroe – he small, fifty-plus, highly intelligent and ill with a bad heart, she thirty years younger and looking, to the casual on-looker, like a typical Hollywood starlet on the make – were seen everywhere. Hyde's wife called her lawyers and started divorce proceedings, with Monroe as 'the other woman', except that she would not see it like that. She did not believe in breaking up marriages (as she would tell press reporters again and again during the course of her career) and it was not her fault Johnny and his wife did not get along any more.

Hyde did not have a lot of material to push with on Marilyn's behalf. There was the part in the very forgettable B-movie, *Ladies of the Chorus*, one line and a swing

of the hips in *Love Happy*, and hundreds of pin-up pictures in American girlie magazines. Not a lot for an agent telling anyone who would listen that the new girl on his list was the greatest yet.

She did get another small part around this time, as one of a troupe of 1870s show girls singing and dancing in *A Ticket to Tomahawk*, but it did not add much to the studios' view of her. She made this one back on the Twentieth Century-Fox lot, and had at least one noticeable scene, a dance routine with the film's leading man, the pleasant Dan Dailey, and three other chorus girls. The number they put across together was called 'Oh, What a Forward Young Man You Are.'

In dancing with Dan Dailey in a Fox Technicolor movie, Monroe was linking

Left *and* below: *Casual and sophisticated images in two more Monroe contributions to the cheesecake market.*

herself with one of the great traditions of the studio, that of the Fox Blonde. In 1950, the title was still held by Betty Grable, the greatest of them all who had had Dan Dailey, a superb dancer, as her leading man in three of her recent pictures, *Mother Wore Tights*, *My Baby Smiles at Me* and *My Blue Heaven*. It was known to the cinema audiences of the day that this sort of fact would get Monroe noticed. Here was a blonde good enough to dance with Dan Dailey – who usually danced with the great and famous Betty Grable. And Monroe was certainly the blondest and the prettiest of the chorus girls on their way to Tomahawk.

Other stars of the film were Anne Baxter, Rory Calhoun, Walter Brennan and a train called Engine One. The film's plot concerned the machinations of a stage-coach owner trying to prevent the train completing its run to Tomahawk in Colorado, and so winning its charter to operate. Anne Baxter was cast in the unlikely part of the granddaughter of the local U.S. Marshal deputizing for the old man as the train's escort on its journey. Dan Dailey and the chorus girls were passengers on the train.

It would not be long before Baxter and Monroe were to meet again on the set of a much more prestigious film altogether.

In the meantime, Johnny Hyde was working away on Marilyn's behalf. Hyde also tried to persuade Marilyn to marry him. She refused. A rich man who knew he did not have much longer to live, he even pointed out to her that she would not have to bother with him long before she would be a widow with the security of a good fortune. Still Marilyn said no. Whatever was motivating the poor little girl from the orphanage and the succession of foster homes, it clearly was not a desire for money. Although she cared considerably for Hyde and, indeed, would be deeply distressed by his death in December 1950, she did not love him and perhaps was still naïvely romantic enough to believe that to

Opposite: The dewy-eyed freshness of youth has given way to a smoother, more sophisticated air in this 1950 glamour shot of Marilyn Monroe, à la Lana Turner.

Right: Another chorus, another pair of fishnet tights for Marilyn, here keeping hatbrim and feathers nicely poised while preparing to dance with Dan Dailey in A Ticket to Tomahawk (1950).

Below: Philippe Halsman photographed this group of hopeful Twentieth Century-Fox contract players in 1950. Is it just hindsight and nostalgia that has us voting Marilyn, in the front row, as the one most likely to make it?

marry someone, you had to love them. Perhaps, too, Hyde simply did not fit into her scheme of things. She wanted to be *someone*, famous in her own right, and marriage to Hyde could reduce her to the status of wife, an appendage to someone else.

Among the good things that Hyde was able to do for Marilyn was to get her a new contract with Twentieth Century-Fox. It was for the usual seven years, at a starting salary of $750 a week. Here, at last, was a secure-looking future. Hyde, a sophisticated and elegant gentleman, also helped with her appearance, toning down the slightly juvenile brassiness and substituting a more smooth, sophisticated look. The latter even extended to her face; her front teeth were straightened a fraction, and an operation cured the slight thickness of the end of her nose. Marilyn was growing up.

She was also growing old – or, at least, too old to be a Hollywood starlet. In 1950, she was in her twenty-fifth year and in Hollywood you can't be a believable starlet at that age: you have either moved up to full actress status or you have gone back home.

Looking about her, Marilyn must have felt some twinges of anxiety. Fortunately, Johnny Hyde got her two good parts.

Good Things Round the Corner

Marilyn Monroe's fifth film appearance, and the one which at last got her an appreciable amount of public attention, came her way mainly because Johnny Hyde's persistence got her an introduction to Metro-Goldwyn-Mayer. Lucille Ryman, a talent scout there, had been impressed by what she saw of Marilyn – having been first alerted to her possibilities on screen after seeing the test Marilyn had done for Ben Lyon at Twentieth Century-Fox.

Not long afterwards, M.G.M. began casting a new film, based on a dramatically realistic novel about crime in the big city. The film was *The Asphalt Jungle* and the director was to be the highly regarded John Huston, whose directing credits already included two films considered by many to be among the best ever made, *The Maltese Falcon* and *The Treasure of the Sierra Madre*. Miss Ryman knew about the film, of course, and what kind of actor was needed for each of the parts.

Miss Ryman had seen just the opening for her, Marilyn later said, not a big part, she told her, but a good one, and Johnny Hyde was to get her an interview with John Huston as quickly as possible. Johnny did and Marilyn saw not only Huston, but also the film's producer, Arthur Hornblow.

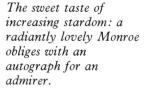

The sweet taste of increasing stardom: a radiantly lovely Monroe obliges with an autograph for an admirer.

The sex goddess clad in form-fitting scarlet is the Monroe image being promoted in the group shot of Hollywood young ones, c. 1950. Others in the photograph are Mitzi Gaynor, Leslie Caron, Tony Curtis and John Derek.

Three or four years later, when Marilyn was 'writing' her autobiography with considerable help from screenwriter and playwright Ben ('The Front Page') Hecht, she dwelt at some length on *The Asphalt Jungle* and how she got her part in it. Her comments were first published when the book was serialized between May and July 1954 in a rather lurid 'popular' British Sunday newspaper, the *Empire News*. Whetting its reader's appetites, the paper announced on April 25: 'Hollywood's most talked-about star, the girl 50,000 men wanted to marry, is writing her own story. FOR THE FIRST TIME. A story that even shock-proof Hollywood is

This 1950 publicity shot of Marilyn depicts her as a poised, perfectly groomed, flawlessly made-up product of the Hollywood machine.

awaiting nervously . . . .' It failed, though, to mention Ben Hecht's part in the book for which the newspaper had bought exclusive British serialization rights.

'Mr. Huston was an exciting looking man,' Marilyn told the *Empire News* readers. 'He was tall, long-faced and his hair was mussed. He was a genius – the first I had ever met.'

The genius with the mussed-up hair gave Marilyn a copy of the film's screenplay, which he had written himself in collaboration with Ben Maddow, and asked her to return for a reading when she had studied it.

Johnny Hyde, when he had seen the script, expressed some concern. 'Do you think you can do it? You have to break up in it, and cry and sob.' Marilyn was determined to do it, and spent several days studying it with Natasha Lytess. She looked not only at the lines she had to read (Angela, the teen-age blonde mistress of one of the criminals in the film) but at the whole script, so that she could assess the relationship between her character and the others.

'I knew the part wouldn't be cut out of the picture because it was vital to the plot. Louis Calhern [whose mistress she played] committed suicide in the story,' she wrote. 'My characterization was Mae West, Theda Bara and Bo-Peep – in tight silk lounging pyjamas.'

Armed with this rather startling vision of the role, she went back to John Huston. The reading turned out to be a memorable one, not least because Monroe did it lying on the floor! As most of the scenes with Angela in them are played with her horizontal, Monroe had done much of her rehearsing with Natasha Lytess lying down. Nervous at the outset of her interview with Huston, she was made even more so by the discovery that Huston had no couch in his office.

Sure that she could not do justice to herself if she read standing up, she found the courage to say she wanted to do her reading lying on the floor. Huston agreed, his assistant director got down on the floor, too, the better to cue her, and Marilyn did her reading. She did not think it was good enough and insisted on doing it again: even with the great director, and even though the part was modest; the 'little nobody' knew her own mind.

Marilyn got Angela's part. It was not a big one, and she had only two major scenes, both with Louis Calhern, but she managed to make them telling, giving Angela, who could have come across as just a cheap, dumb blonde, a certain sensitivity. She looked stunning, too, very svelte and sophisticated.

'In a movie, you act in little bits and pieces,' she – or Ben Hecht – wrote in the *Empire News*. 'You say two lines and they say "cut". They set up the camera in another place and you say two more lines. You walk five feet, and they "cut." The minute you get going good in your characterization they cut.

'But it doesn't matter. There's no audience watching you. There's nobody to act *for* except yourself. It's like the games you play when you are a child and pretend to be someone else. Usually, it's almost the same sort of story you made up as a child . . .

'I didn't have this daydream while making *Asphalt Jungle* because it was an

'Bo Peep in tight silk lounging pyjamas' was how Monroe described her interpretation of the part of Angela in The Asphalt Jungle *(1950). Watching her lounging to good effect is Louis Calhern and an assortment of film crew members.*

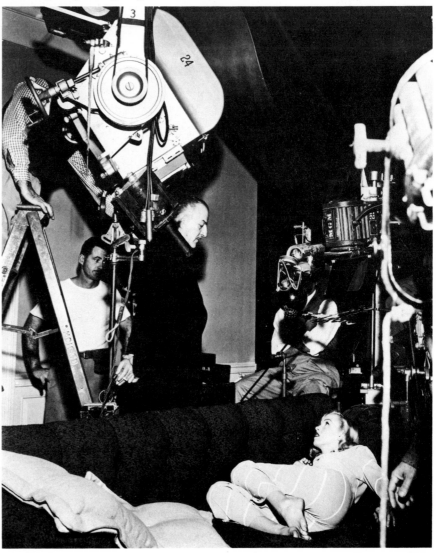

adult script. There was also an audience watching me, an audience of one, the director. A director like John Huston makes your work exciting. Some directors seem more interested in photographing the scenery than the actors . . . . Mr. Huston wasn't like that. He was interested in my acting, even though my role was a minor one.'

It seemed so minor, in fact, that Marilyn's name was left off the list of credits when the film was sneak-previewed. The audience reaction to her was so positive and so many people asked on their preview comment cards who the young blonde was, that she was added to the credits.

The Asphalt Jungle was released by Metro-Goldwyn-Mayer early in 1950 and was an instant critical success, as much for the realism of Huston's handling of its dramatic and serious theme as for the acting of its fine cast.

The film tells the story of how a gang of petty city criminals plan to relieve a jewellers' shop of a million dollars-worth of its stock, getting rid of the proceeds via a smooth and crooked lawyer called Alonzo Emmerich (Louis Calhern), a known fence. The raid is conceived and planned by a recently released prisoner, Doc Riedenschneider (Sam Jaffe, giving such a strong performance he was nominated for a best supporting actor Oscar). Among the gang he gets together are Dix Handley (Sterling Hayden), who wants the money to enable him to buy back his family's farm in Kentucky, a hunchback driver called Gus (James Whitmore) and a safe-breaker, Louis (Anthony Caruso). Things go wrong almost from the beginning, when Louis is accidentally shot by a night watchman who comes across them after they have raided the store. Then, when they get to Emmerich's office with the jewels, they find he does not have the

Marilyn Monroe as crook's mistress/'niece', Angela, in John Huston's The Asphalt Jungle.

money to pay them. In fact, Emmerich always knew that he would not be able to raise the money and had planned to double-cross them from the outset, using his beautiful blonde 'niece' Angela to help him convince the gang of his good intentions.

During the inevitable argument in Emmerich's office after the robbery, one of the lawyer's crooked associates is shot and Handley is seriously wounded. When the police find the corpse of Emmerich's henchman, arrests soon follow. When Angela does not back up Emmerich's lying story, he commits suicide rather than face receiving a long prison sentence. Handley himself escapes arrest with the aid of Doll (Jean Hagen), the good girl who loves him, but he eventually dies of his wounds.

Where *The Asphalt Jungle* stood out from other crime movies was in its realistic and even sympathetic treatment of the criminals. The gang, under Huston's handling, were not just cardboard figures set up to carry out the requirements of the plot. They were men with homes and families, with emotions and sympathies that dictated their actions and even, especially in the case of the safe-breaker, Louis, with a professional pride in their jobs. Huston's camerawork ensured his audiences appreciated the men's emotions, and the part they played in their actions, by using close-ups to great effect. These were real people, who could smile at a cat or at a girl dancing, with whom audiences could identify – which made their inevitable failure and death all the more poignant. Yes, the film was saying, crime does not pay, but we may still regret the destruction of the criminals.

The film was highly popular with audiences on both sides of the Atlantic and was an instant critical success, garnering enthusiastic reviews for both John Huston's taut and dramatic direction and for the performances of its cast, including Monroe, whom *Photoplay* magazine said made the most of her footage, and whom others described as 'luscious', 'exciting' and even 'dazzling'.

As well as Sam Jaffe's Academy Award nomination, John Huston also received two, for best screenplay and best director. *The Asphalt Jungle* was undoubtedly one of the best films of 1950, a year that also

saw such vintage pieces as *Sunset Boulevard* and *Born Yesterday*, and might even have collected itself an Oscar or two if it had not been for *All About Eve*, Marilyn's next film, which was released in 1950 and which did gather in the Academy Awards – six of them.

Twentieth Century-Fox were making this film, and director/writer Joseph Mankiewicz and Johnny Hyde had to do quite a lot of persuasive talking to get Darryl Zanuck to agree to Monroe's being in it. Most of Hyde's initial talking was done to Mankiewicz, who had liked Monroe's work in *The Asphalt Jungle* and who thought she might be better in the small but not insignificant part of Miss Caswell than the other young actresses he had been

Precariously balanced, Monroe still manages a carefree smile in one of her early official starlet portraits at Twentieth Century-Fox. This one was released as part of the promotion for All About Eve.

Party guests assembled on the staircase of Margo Channing's apartment in All About Eve *(1950): Gregory Ratoff, Anne Baxter, Gary Merrill, Marilyn Monroe, George Sanders and Celeste Holm.*

interviewing. 'There was a breathlessness and a sort of glued-on innocence about her that I found appealing,' he told writer Gary Carey some years later when the latter was interviewing Mankiewicz for his book *More About All About Eve*, published in 1972.

But Mankiewicz was not particularly worried whether he had Monroe or not, and it was Hyde who had to do all the hard work with a reluctant Twentieth Century-Fox. Eventually, he managed to negotiate her now contract for her (although even he had to be content with a six-month option clause in it), and to persuade the studio to take her fully back into the fold by giving her a part in a decent film.

All About Eve turned out to be much more than 'decent', of course. With six Oscars (Best Film, Best Screenplay, Best Director, Best Supporting Actor, Best Costume Design and Best Sound Recording) to its credit and many other awards as well, the film is for many one of Hollywood's finest. A brilliantly witty, highly sophisticated look at the bitchery that goes on backstage in the live theatre, *All About Eve* is also a fine study of the relationship between men and women in general, and between that very special

kind of female, the stage actress, and the men and women around her in particular.

Joseph Mankiewicz, whose screenplay for the film and his directing of it, won two of the film's Oscars (establishing a record, for he had won the same two Academy Awards the year before for *A Letter to Three Wives*), based his screenplay on a story called 'The Wisdom of Eve' by actress and playwright Mary Orr. There were many significant departures from Miss Orr's story in the Mankiewicz treatment, however, particularly in his handling of the characters, and Mankiewicz did not hesitate to add characters of his own to give flesh to the bones of the story. He also shaped the whole thing as a series of flashbacks within the framework of a prize-giving ceremony, so that the pursuit of awards, and the often hollow victory that results, became another theme of the film. But his greatest move away from the short story was in his re-creation of the main female part, that of Margo Channing who in Mankiewicz's version is a successful, brilliant, unmarried actress who has now reached forty: the great divide, which separates actresses who can play ingénues and young lovers from those who no longer can. She is, moreover, in love with

Left: *Margo Channing (Bette Davis) makes sure Eve (Anne Baxter) and theatre critic Addison DeWitt (George Sanders) are acquainted in* All About Eve. *Beautiful dumb blonde Miss Caswell (Marilyn Monroe) looks on.*

Left: *Hollywood glamour, early 1950s variety. Marilyn with roses.*

a man eight years younger than herself. Though she does not know it yet, waiting in the wings, ready to step out on the centre of the stage and snatch her career from her – and perhaps much else besides – is Eve Harrington.

Bette Davis gave one of the greatest performances of a long and distinguished film career as Margo Channing, and Anne Baxter played the part of Eve Harrington with a perfect mixture of sweet humility and steely predatoriness.

Marilyn Monroe's Miss Caswell was a minor part, on the fringes of the action, but it was an important one for it offered yet another view of the female in quest of a career on the stage. Miss Caswell's problem was that she had looks but no talent; she was predatory, too, but her inner character was so much dead wood. Unlike Eve, who was a superb actress, on and off stage, she was dumb, she could not act, and she was going nowhere.

Monroe managed to project all this very effectively, especially in her biggest scene in the film (the long set piece, in fact, which all true 'Eve' fanatics can quote verbatim at the drop of a hat). There is a party at Margo Channing's house, plenty of hired help on hand – summed up by

Margo's dresser and confidant Birdie (marvellously played by Thelma Ritter) as 'some loose characters dressed like maids and butlers' – and the atmosphere crackles with static from the start. Margo has just made her famous statement from the staircase about fastening your seatbelts, 'it's going to be a bumpy night,' when there arrives waspish, acerbic drama critic Addison DeWitt (played with enormous presence by George Sanders: he won the Best Supporting Actor Oscar for his efforts) with his 'protégée', Miss Caswell, who is, he tells Margo, 'A graduate of the Copacabana School of Dramatic Arts.' We could have guessed this for ourselves, for Miss Claudia Caswell's lovely face, framed by elegant, swept-back blonde hair and long earrings, does not suggest the intelligence needed to be a good actress, while her well-curved figure sheathed in a tight gown and draped with fur suggests quite other things. DeWitt treats her condescendingly, dismissively throughout. Later, Miss Caswell, desperate for a drink, hails a passing servant, 'Oh, waiter . . .' She is ignored. 'That isn't a waiter, my dear. That's a butler,'

The bobby-soxer image is not all that unlikely in this picture of Marilyn and adoring students, since she did enrol for classes at the University of Southern California in the early 1950s.

DeWitt points out. 'I can't yell "Oh, butler," can I? Maybe somebody's name is Butler,' Miss Caswell replies with exquisite reasonableness.

All About Eve was premièred in New York in October 1950. Critical reaction was more or less unanimously enthusiastic for every aspect of the film.

Bosley Crowther, in the *New York Times*, talked about the 'dazzling and devastating mockery that is brilliantly packed into this film' and singled Bette Davis out of 'a truly sterling cast' for special mention.

Time magazine called *Eve* a 'needle-sharp study of bitchery in the Broadway theatre . . . probably Hollywood's closest original approach to the bite, sheen and wisdom of high comedy' and, having noted Bette Davis' performance in particular, summed up by saying that *All About Eve* should please film-goers who valued the kind of grown-up, pithy entertainment all too seldom found in films.

The *New York Herald Tribune*, describing the film as a supremely adroit and professional piece of cinema artistry, said that individual performances, all of the same high quality, stand out only in size.

Over in England, where the British Film Academy was to give *All About Eve* its award for the best film from any source shown in Britain in 1950, the *Daily Express* opined that it would be the 'top talkie' of the year on sheer merit, and that the dazzling dialogue and the savagery of its observation would make it a pace-setter.

In Britain, as in the United States, the film was shown in scheduled performances rather than in continuous screenings; Darryl Zanuck, treating the film as if it were a true stage performance, decreed that latecomers were not to be admitted.

There were two drawbacks in all this as far as Marilyn Monroe's screen career were concerned. Firstly, the cast of *All About Eve* were all so effective that, apart from Bette Davis and George Sanders, critics were inclined not to single out individual performances; thus Marilyn received few specific notices for her performance. Secondly, this was yet another film in which she had played a 'dumb blonde'. True, there were subtle and well-drawn differences between her characterizations of this part and that of Angela in

The Asphalt Jungle, but few people noticed them.

Johnny Hyde did, but Hyde's weak heart finally gave out on him and he died just before Christmas 1950. Marilyn wept openly at his funeral, and said years afterwards that she had never stopped missing him. She never again had anyone whose advice about her career she could rely on so utterly as she had with Johnny; as an actress making her way in a desperately hard profession she was now very much on her own.

Perhaps in an attempt to live up to Johnny Hyde's idealized view of her, she decided around this time to do something about her mind. She was not dumb, although she had acquired a dumb-blonde image, but she knew she was woefully ignorant. 'I realized that two-thirds of the time I had no idea what people were talking about,' she wrote for the *Empire News*, so she enrolled in an art and literature appreciation course at the University of Southern California.

'I discovered the Renaissance, met Michelangelo, Raphael and Tintoretto. Then there was not enough time.' Poor Marilyn.

'Finally,' she wrote with amusing, rather heart-touching naïvety, 'I decided

Beauty and the book: Marilyn dons sweater, shorts and high heels to cavort below a shelf-full of books for this early 1950s pin-up.

Opposite: *By the early 1950s Marilyn Monroe was becoming the sort of girl who gets photographed in public places even when doing the most ordinary things.*

Below: *Roller derby enthusiasts Monroe, James Brown and Mickey Rooney cheer on the team in a scene from* The Fireball *(1950).*

to postpone my intelligence, but I made a promise to myself I won't forget. I promised that in a few years time when everything had settled down I would start learning – everything. I would read all the books and find out about all the wonders there were in the world.'

She usually did find time to read books, several people commenting on the surprisingly (to them) intellectual nature of the books she would read on set, and she was a reasonably familiar figure in the Pickwick bookshop on Hollywood Boulevard, where she liked to browse until she found something that looked interesting.

As it turned out, things never would settle down for her, and most of the world's wonders were left undiscovered. Looking at the next few films she made,

though, it would not be surprising to learn that, despite *Asphalt Jungle* and *All About Eve*, she was still afraid that her career might not, even now, take off.

It wasn't that she didn't believe in herself – 'I knew I belonged to the public and to the world, not because I was talented or even beautiful but because I had never belonged to anything or anyone else' – it was just that Twentieth Century-Fox in general and Darryl F. Zanuck in particular showed no sign that they thought so, too.

For weeks she sat about doing nothing. No parts were offered her, no casting directors put her name on a list. Perhaps the very ordinary films she had appeared in around her two good films in 1950 affected their judgement.

One of them, *The Fireball*, was a misnomer if ever there was one, for this tale of roller-skating speedway, made by an independent production company and released by Fox a few months or so before *All About Eve*, was a fairly tame affair. Mickey Rooney, now approaching thirty and grabbing any parts he could get to pay off the debts of his failed production company, had the lead part of Johnny Casar, a boy who runs away from the orphanage where he has been brought up to try to make an independent life for himself. Pat O'Brien, former good guy of many a Warners 'social conscience' film, and star of at least one highly regarded film with a sporting theme, *Knute Rockne – All American*, was brought in, no doubt to lend authority to the proceedings, to

play Father O'Hara, the priest who runs the orphanage and continues to keep an eye on Johnny – to be the guardian of his soul, as it were – as the boy's career in roller skating takes off.

Johnny is taught how to skate by a pretty young champion roller skater, Mary Reeves (Beverly Tyler) who befriends him at a Rollerbowl. Soon Johnny has learned enough to begin winning races (or, as the scriptwriters will have it, 'Crashing to the top on screaming wheels'). Father O'Hara and Mary are proud of him until his achievements start going to his head and he becomes too full of himself to bother about the rest of the team with whom he is supposed to be skating. Hints about Christian humility from Father O'Hara are ignored, as is sweet, loving Mary in favour of a succession of women interested in him not for himself but for his success. Which was where Marilyn Monroe came in, for she had the part of one of the predatory women, a rather tarty blonde called Polly.

Eventually, as is the way in these cinematic morality plays, retribution descends on Johnny in the form of polio, from which he recovers after loving nursing care from Mary. He rejoins the team, demonstrating that he has finally learned to be unselfish and consider others before himself, by helping a younger member of his team to win the big race which, not so long before, he would have gone all out to win for his personal glorification. Johnny, in fact, has learned humility, and this regains him the regard of Father O'Hara and the true love of Mary.

Since *The Fireball* was directed by Tay Garnett, an experienced film-maker who generally managed to bring a good measure of authenticity to his plots and characters, it was not exactly a bad film; it just did not have very much for the viewers to get excited about, apart from some fairly colourful and action-packed racing sequences.

It had also been tightly budgeted. Clearly, it was one of those B-movies where the actors provide most of their own costume. Marilyn had obviously had to rummage through her own cupboards: the sleeveless knitted pullover she wears over a long-sleeved black blouse in one of her race-watching scenes with Mickey Rooney turns up again in a later film, *Hometown Story*.

Marilyn appeared in another film in 1950, *Right Cross*, which was also made at M.G.M. In it she had a very small and unbilled part as a beautiful and sophisticated-looking woman who has a drink in a nightclub with Dick Powell (playing a sports reporter concerned for the future welfare of a boxer with a failing right hand). Ricardo Montalban was the boxer and M.G.M.'s favourite girl-next-door, June Allyson, was his girlfriend. Lionel Barrymore also appeared in the film as the boxer's fight promoter. A good cast, then, and nicely directed by John Sturges. The reviews were not bad, but nobody took much notice of Marilyn.

The film's main interest today for Monroe fans lies in the fact that it marks another step on the path from the rather

Inimitable Monroe version of a 'head and shoulders' shot, dating from the early 1950s.

Marilyn had a tiny part as an elegant blonde in a nightclub in Right Cross *(1950). Here, she seems to be the only one with a drink at a table shared with Dick Powell.*

brassy girl she was at the outset of her film career towards the more assured woman she became in the early 1950s.

No doubt it was mostly her own efforts, with some advice from friends, especially Johnny Hyde, though Marilyn was to tell a story of how that great lady Miss Joan Crawford once tried to take a hand in dressing her.

'It is so easy not to look vulgar,' Miss Crawford is supposed to have intoned. 'The main thing about dressing well is to see that everything you wear is just right, that your shoes, stockings, gloves and bag all fit the suit you are wearing. What I

would like you to do,' she went on with breath-taking impertinence, 'is to make a list of all the clothes in your wardrobe and I'll make a list of all the things you need to buy and see you buy the right things.'

Marilyn never did make the list, which is perhaps why Miss Crawford, Marilyn's disobedience still rankling, later publicly expressed her disgust at the vulgarly sexy gown Marilyn chose to wear at one of Hollywood's great prize-giving occasions. And perhaps Marilyn's telling of the ridiculous story of Joan Crawford, dress adviser, was her way of getting back at the latter for her public telling-off.

Marilyn had a part in one more M.G.M. film, *Home Town Story*, before she returned to Twentieth Century-Fox. Her part was still small, but she was much more in evidence than she had been in *Right Cross*.

Home Town Story, with a running time of a mere 61 minutes, was one of those B-movies usually intended as the first half of a double bill. Since the same man who wrote the story and screenplay, Arthur Pierson, also produced and directed the film, it is reasonable to assume that he had a certain amount of faith in it, though the rather dismissive notices the film achieved in the papers indicate that faith was not enough. Marilyn Monroe and the other players were said to be 'up to script demands', but since they also described the script as being 'short and simple – at

The world's view of Marilyn Monroe in the early 1950s: a beautiful blonde projecting an enormous sex appeal.

times almost too simple', this was not saying a great deal.

Home Town Story was based on the hoary old theme that has been the staple of B movies since they started making them – that of the crusading newspaperman fighting the forces of darkness, in this case, the inhumanity of big business.

The newspaperman was Blake Washburn, played by Jeffrey Lynn, a former Warners leading player and a more than competent actor with many films to his credit. Blake has returned to his home town after being defeated in an attempt to get re-elected to the state legislature by the son of a rich manufacturer. Settling in, he agrees to take over the editorship of the local paper from his uncle, who is retiring. Providing secretarial assistance in the newspaper office is attractive blonde Iris Martin (Monroe), always competently and decoratively on hand with notebook and well-sharpened pencil to take down the boss's every word. Miss Martin sported a smooth hair style and elegant turnout, including well-fitting sweaters, which suggested that either Monroe or the M.G.M. costume and make-up people had taken as their model their most famous blonde pin-up star, the lovely Sweater Girl, Lana Turner.

Blake, his judgement impaired by disappointment, decides that the influence of the rich manufacturer, John MacFarlane (played by Donald Crisp), upon the election has been a bad one, perhaps even dishonest, and begins using the newspaper to run a campaign against him and the evils of big business.

In the end, when his little sister's life has been saved by machinery manufactured in MacFarlane's factory, Blake comes to his senses and realizes that big business can be an influence for good in the world after all.

Home Town Story was released by M.G.M. in May 1951, a year that had begun none too auspiciously for Marilyn, with Johnny Hyde's death overshadowing her private life. She did not sit around and mope, however. Her college art-appreciation course was taken seriously – at first, anyway – and she went back to the old routine of cheesecake photography for publicity purposes: if Darryl F. Zanuck was not going to let the public see her on screen, then they sure as hell would see her in as many magazines and papers as

A lobby card for Home Town Story *(1951), in which Monroe played one of her several 'secretary with notebook and pencil' parts.*

she could get herself into. 'I wouldn't be forgotten in a year,' she vowed. 'The public was the only family, the only Prince Charming and the only home I had ever dreamed about', sentiments here quoted from the *Empire News* that she made sure the public knew about, for she was always good at keeping in close touch with the studio's publicity people and with the men and women who filled the gossip columns the American film-going public read so avidly. One columnist particularly close to her was Sidney Skolsky, and he was one of the best.

Monroe's publicity policy paid off, and her fan mail at the studio began to increase noticeably. The Korean War probably helped: it created a big market for pin-ups, and since Betty Grable, Lana Turner, Rita Hayworth and their like were clearly no longer of an age to be the most popular pin-ups of this War as they had been of World War II, Marilyn Monroe stepped into their elegant, high-heeled shoes.

She was sensational. Line up her pin-ups next to Grable's, and the difference hits you between the eyes. Grable in stills looks like a doll – pretty and very shapely, to be sure, but with not much more life

Marilyn poised to take notes from Alan Hale Jr. in a scene from Home Town Story. *Marilyn's blouse and sleeveless sweater had already been given an airing in* The Fireball.

58

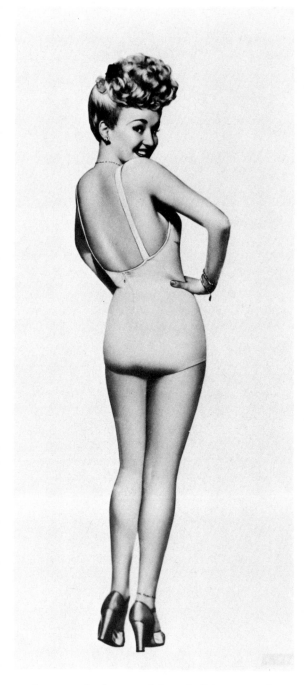

and warmth than a china doll in a toyshop window, out of reach, not to be touched. Monroe's vitality, her sheer joy in life, her obvious delight in her own gorgeous shape, reaches out of every picture. 'Let's enjoy life together,' she seems to be saying. The response from the great American public, or at least the masculine part of it, was resounding and enthusiastic and was reaching the studio in the form of sacks of fan mail, and of expressions of considerable interest from film distributors and cinema managers.

1951 was some months old before the moguls of Twentieth Century-Fox got an inkling of what was happening. According to established Monroe mythology what finally opened their eyes was the sight of a collection of their most celebrated stars, gathered together to show the flag at an important meeting of Fox distributors and cinema managers, being swept aside as a roomful of red-blooded males tried to get close to Marilyn. It was the eyes of the top Fox Mogul, company president Spyros Skouras, that opened the widest. Acting fast and with a skill perhaps acquired when he had been a poor shepherd boy in Greece, Skouras detached Monroe from the mob, sat her down beside him at the top table, and started finding out about this unknown asset.

The next day the word went forth: Marilyn Monroe was to be put into any current Fox movie that had a part suited

Opposite: All those acting lessons pay off for Marilyn as she and Wally Brown emote surprise and astonishment in a scene from As Young As You Feel *(1951).*

Left: Marilyn did not get star billing on the posters for As Young As You Feel, *but a slinky black dress drew attention to her shapely presence.*

to her talents and blonde loveliness. Her contract was also to be put on much firmer foundations than Johnny Hyde and his William Morris Agency had been able to negotiate.

The first film Fox found for her was *As Young As You Feel*, an insignificant movie with comic pretensions. It turned out to be entertaining enough as something to keep the audience quiet while they were waiting for the big picture in the second half. *As Young As You Feel* was a 'dualer', in fact, but that was about all. Probably Marilyn was too relieved to be in work at Twentieth Century-Fox again, and with a proper contract at her back, to worry about the quality of the film, or her part in it. At least she was practised in her role, for she was playing a secretary again, armed with a spiral-bound notebook and a handful of lethally sharpened pencils. She looked pretty luscious, too, especially when she wore a very unsecretarial low-fronted dress, for Fox had softened the smooth Lana-like hairstyle of *Home Town Story*, and had used clever make-up to give her a dewy, wide-eyed look. She also had enough scenes in the film to get herself noticed.

With names like Monty Woolley, Thelma Ritter, Constance Bennett, David Wayne and Albert Dekker all lurking in the cast list – as was that of the youthful Roger Moore, getting in some practice for his much later James Bond roles – Marilyn at least had some fine talent to watch while she waited for her own scenes.

As Young As You Feel concerns the machinations of sixty-five-year-old John Hodges (Monty Woolley) to get his job back when he is forcibly retired, due to company policy. Only his granddaughter Alice (Jean Peters) shows any real concern for John Hodges's plight when he tells his family of his retirement. Alice probably has reason for sympathizing with anyone wishing to remain with Acme Printing Services, as she is in love with Joe (David Wayne), who works in the company's personnel department.

Discovering that Acme's retirement policy is dictated by the parent company, Consolidated Motors, Hodges devises a plan to get his job back which involves him in impersonating Consolidated's chairman, Mr. Cleveland.

Acme's boss, Louis McKinley (Albert Dekker) is considerably disturbed to learn

61

that 'Cleveland' intends visiting his company to see that all is going well, and not even the cooing, sweetly comforting presence of his secretary, Harriet (Monroe), reassures him.

Naturally, complications arise. McKinley's wife (Constance Bennett) falls in love with the black-bearded 'Cleveland' and goes so far as to leave her husband. The real Cleveland turns up, offering Hodges a big job at Acme; poor McKinley, trying to order his wife home, looses off some nasty remarks at the real Cleveland, which does his standing at Acme no good. There is, of course, a happy ending, with all the tangles smoothed out.

Some of the film's reviews were quite enthusiastic, Bosley Crowther in the *New York Times* going so far as to say that Monroe was 'superb' in her part, which was perhaps a bit exaggerated, but the notice must have been sweet music to Marilyn's ear.

From this film, Monroe went into another less-than-important Fox comedy,

Love Nest. The credit list was lengthy, but Marilyn got fourth billing and big size type on the posters and the film's title-credits. Someone, somewhere had decided her stock should rise a bit.

June Haver and William Lundigan starred in *Love Nest*, and this would be the penultimate film in Haver's career: a 'nice' girl, she never quite looked as if she had what it would take to replace Betty Grable as top Fox Blonde, as the studio had hoped at the outset of her career. In 1953, Haver retired from her film career and after trying the life of a nun in a convent finally settled for marriage with Fred MacMurray. By then, of course, Monroe was the one who was ousting Grable, and even in *Love Nest*, she looked as if she could do it: she seemed so much more sparkling, even in a small role, than the quieter, even mousey, Haver.

William Lundigan's career followed a pattern not dissimilar from that other B-movie stalwart, Ronald Reagan (apart from the politics). Like Reagan, Lundigan started out as a radio announcer, coming

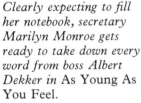

Clearly expecting to fill her notebook, secretary Marilyn Monroe gets ready to take down every word from boss Albert Dekker in As Young As You Feel.

to Hollywood, where he played 'nice-guy' roles, at the end of the 1930s. In the mid-1950s he gave his career and public standing a fillip by hosting a television series – and acting as public spokesman for the sponsoring company – just as Reagan had done. About the only other name to stand out in a fairly un-distinguished cast list is that of Jack Paar, whose later great fame was to come through television, not the cinema.

The 'love nest' of the film's title is an old house in New York in which returning

G.I. Jim Scott (Lundigan) finds that his wife Connie (Haver) has invested their savings. Jim wants to be a writer, and Connie reckons they should be able to get enough money from renting rooms in the house to tide them over until Jim's books start bringing in the cash.

Unfortunately, the house is more than a little dilapidated and all the necessary repairs and noise prevents Jim from getting down to his novel, while his friends who move in don't come up with all that much rent.

Singalong round the piano for Frank Fay (left), Marilyn Monroe, Jack Paar (playing the piano) and friends in Love Nest.

Further distraction arrives in the comely shape of ex-WAC Roberta Stevens (Monroe) who knew Jim in their army days and now takes a room in the house, where another of Jim's old friends, lawyer Ed Forbes (Jack Paar) is also lurking. Ed likes the looks of Roberta very much: Connie does not. Thus a bit of tension is introduced into the plot.

The house just about lives up to its title of 'love nest' when one of the tenants, Charlie Patterson (Frank Fay) marries another, Eadie Gaynor (Leatrice Joy). But Charlie fetches up in jail for parting rich widows from their money, and manages to get Jim ensnared with him. While in jail, the two settle down to getting Charlie's hair-raising life story on paper, the resulting memoirs, when published, making money for them both. So all turns out for the best in this best of all possible worlds.

A pretty feeble plot, to be sure, and an on the whole rather ordinary cast to try to put it across. It is not surprising that its only bright spot now seems to be Marilyn.

Even at the time, she used it to put down her marker. In such costumes as an itsy-bitsy polka dot bikini or a distractingly low-cut black evening gown, she certainly catches the eye.

With *Love Nest*, the archetypal Monroe is emerging, like a butterfly from a chrysalis. The eyes, under their heavy, dark eyebrows and fringed with false eyelashes, are losing their little girl innocence – though she could still turn this on when necessary – and are now offering languorous, side-long glances under heavy lids. The provocative beauty spot on her left cheek is now allowed to show, emphasizing the corner of her mouth, which is more often than not open to give a glimpse of her strong, white teeth. We are seeing rather more of the richly curved, sexy body, too. She even has a scene in which she undresses, down to her underwear. The boys in the back row must have loved it.

As part of the publicity campaign for *Love Nest*, Zanuck issued the firm statement that Marilyn Monroe was the most exciting new personality Hollywood had seen in a long time. He probably did not believe it, but out in the big wide world, lots of people did.

At least Fox did not let up on her. From *Love Nest*, she went straight into work on another rather feeble comedy, *Let's Make It Legal*, a vehicle for the faltering career of the sophisticated comedienne Claudette Colbert. A year before she should have been Margo Channing in *All About Eve*, but an accident that severely damaged her back let Bette Davis into that film and also, seemingly, sent her own career down a path marked by increasingly unworthy films.

Colbert had two male co-stars in this film, Zachary Scott and Macdonald Carey, and there were two more players, Robert Wagner and Barbara Bates, before Monroe's name was reached on the credits list. Although her part was incidental to the plot, it allowed her to appear in a succession of eye-catching strapless evening gowns, bathing costumes and skimpy shorts.

The plot of *Let's Make It Legal* turned on the two-men-love-the-same-girl theme. Man Number One is Hugh (Macdonald Carey) husband of twenty-years standing to Miriam (Colbert) who, fed up with his gambling ways, divorces him. Along comes Man Number Two, Victor (Zachary Scott) who has loved Miriam these twenty years, but lost her to Hugh on the roll of a dice. At least, he swears he has loved Miriam, but his love turns out to be a feeble thing when compared with the strong flame that still burns within Hugh. The latter, in an effort to make Miriam jealous and re-kindle her love for him, takes up with the beautiful blonde Joyce (Monroe), who is staying at the grand hotel where he is public relations chief. Joyce is a lady on the make, the object of

Marilyn's role in Let's Make It Legal *(1951) may have been small, but with her shapely figure clad in form-fitting gowns like this, she was certainly noticeable. Here, she keeps Macdonald Carey supplied with alcoholic stimulant during a late-night poker game.*

Dance floor disagreement for husband Macdonald Carey and ex-wife Claudette Colbert in Let's Make It Legal. *Looking as if their toes are being trodden on in the middle are Marilyn Monroe and Zachary Scott.*

her interest being the rich Victor and the millions he has made out of American industry.

In the end, Hugh gets Miriam back, though probably not too many people in the film's audiences cared very much one way or the other. Despite her small part, Marilyn got friendly notices in several papers, an indication that she was becoming a movie personality to be reckoned with.

Love Nest and *Let's Make It Legal* were both released by Twentieth Century-Fox in October 1951, and cinema audiences would have to wait a long seven months before they could see the increasingly popular Marilyn Monroe on the screen in a new film. In the meantime they, and, it seemed, the whole Western world and probably a few bits behind the Iron Curtain as well, had two very juicy stories about her to consider.

The first one, which should have ended the career of an aspiring actress in the early 1950s, was, of course, those calendars. She had posed for Tom Kelley in 1949, taken her $50 and forgotten about the whole thing. Then late in 1951 the pictures turned up on next year's calendars. They, especially the stretched-out-on-velvet one, looked pretty good and soon began to appear on garage workshop walls all over the country. It was not long before someone noticed the uncanny resemblance between the girl on the calendar and Hollywood's newest blonde sensation.

It took a criminal mind to set the ball rolling. The film Marilyn had recently completed and which was due for release in May 1952 was *Clash by Night*, a powerful drama with a fine cast, which was being produced over at R.K.O., where the production heads were Norman

Krasna and Jerry Walds. Less than two months before the film's release date, Wald started getting telephone calls from someone demanding a large sum of money for not telling the newspapers that one of the stars of *Clash by Night* had been offending 'public morality' by posing nude for calendar pictures, a story that could get the film banned from cinemas across the country. Wald, knowing how sensitive Hollywood had to be about 'morality', public or otherwise, was pretty worried. The dreaded Hays Code was still very much a force to be reckoned with, and most film stars had a morality clause in their contracts that studios could use to keep their players in order. Nevertheless, he was not such a weak character as to give in to blackmail without a struggle. Anyway, even if he paid this one off, what was to stop another blackmailer from trying the same trick? If Monroe was that recognizable, it would not be long before others were noticing too. Finally, he and Krasna came to the conclusion that attack being the best form of defence, they would themselves arrange for the story to be revealed. They tipped off a United Press writer, who called Twentieth Century-Fox's publicity head.

Some friendly advice on camera angles for Marilyn from operative cameraman Fred Bently on the set of Clash by Night.

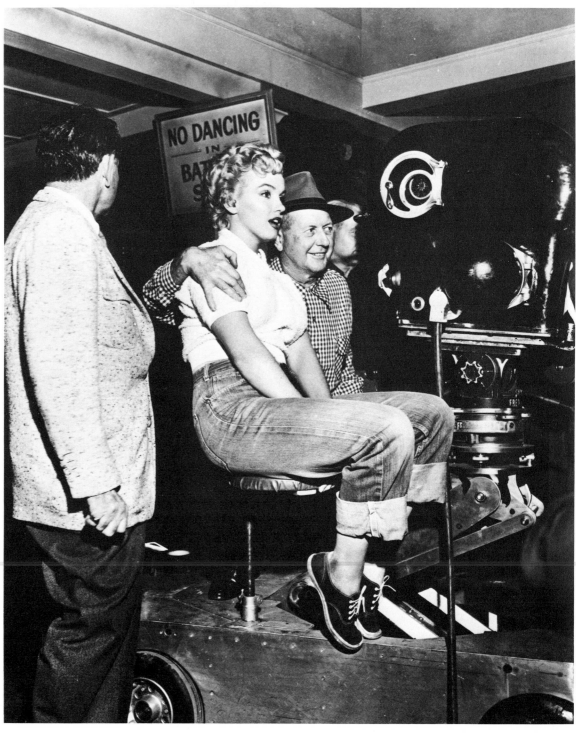

68

Monroe and Keith Andes provided the young love interest in RKO's steamy melodrama Clash by Night *(1952).*

Soon, the Fox studio was in a state of near-hysterical turmoil. Monroe was to be sacked, her latest film would be scrapped, she must deny the whole thing. Monroe wept, but kept her head. She needed some outside advice and called that wise old bird of journalism Sidney Skolsky. He advised her to tell the truth. She did, though with reservations, for she played up the poor, lonely girl hungry in the cruel city bit and neglected to mention the expensive car she had been trying to wrest out of the clutches of the bailiffs.

She won hands down. There were no outraged repercussions from morality groups, her stock of public regard soared, and *Clash by Night* did great business.

The Fox publicity people had hardly got their tin hats and flak jackets back in the cupboard when the second story, one that was potentially even more damaging for Marilyn, broke. Gladys suddenly turned up, not in person but via rumours that began to leak out about the middle-aged woman in the California sanatorium who kept saying, between bouts of Bible reading, that she was Marilyn Monroe's mother.

Once again the studio was in turmoil, for they had been playing the beautiful but sad orphan routine to good effect, and now here was a mother turning up. What sort of a girl was she who could deny her own mother? Once again Marilyn sweet-talked her way out of the danger, telling eager journalists that she had not known of her mother's life in hospital until she herself had grown up and that recently she had been in touch and was doing what she could to help Gladys.

1952 was turning out to be an action-packed year for the public relations people at Fox, who must have felt that protecting the interests of rising star Marilyn Monroe was going to be a job fraught with dangers and hair-breadth escapes. It was clear that world-wide interest in her was high – extraordinarily so, considering that she had not yet made a film in which she had had anything better than a small role. It was clear, too, that she was something of a phenomenon in Hollywood.

Then in May, R.K.O. released *Clash by Night*, and Marilyn Monroe was seen to have more possibilities as an on-screen presence than had hitherto been revealed.

The big stars of *Clash by Night* were Barbara Stanwyck, Paul Douglas and Robert Ryan, playing the three sides of a triangle of love, marriage and adultery. Even on the set, it was Monroe rather than these three established players who was the object of the vociferous attention of journalists, gossip-column writers and photographers. There would come a time when newspapers would be strictly barred

Monroe's way with a glass of beer and her fetching black top attract Robert Ryan's eye in this scene from Clash by Night.

from the sets of Monroe films, but not yet. The Fox publicity machine was clearly working at full steam ahead on the promotion of the girl who only a few months before had not had much more significance in their eyes than might be expected of the holder of the 'Miss Cheesecake 1951' title.

Twentieth Century-Fox had also tacitly acknowledged that perhaps there was something in Monroe's insistence that she was not just a dumb blonde. In 1951 she had been reported as saying that she wanted to be a serious actress, emphatically rejecting the suggestion that she might be Hollywood's new Jean Harlow, a suggestion still doing the rounds in 1952 when Leonard Mosley, a leading London feature writer, pinpointed in the *Daily Express* three contenders for Jean Harlow's crown: Marilyn Monroe, Gloria Grahame and Corinne Calvet. Now, she was being allowed to have her own drama coach, Natasha Lytess, on set. After *Clash by Night*, all of Monroe's directors were going to have to come to terms with her coach on the sideline: some did not.

Monroe's part in *Clash by Night* hardly required the services of a drama coach, for it was fairly slight, even though she had fourth billing. She was cast as a young fish-cannery worker, Peggy, in love with a young man, Joe (Keith Andes), whose elder sister Mae (Stanwyck) has returned to her small home town, a fishing port, bitter and disillusioned after many years away in more sophisticated parts.

Although the film, based on the play of the same name by prolific Broadway playwright Clifford Odets, concentrated on the efforts of Mae to find love and contentment, first in marriage to down-to-earth fishing boat owner Jerry (Paul Douglas) and then in the arms of the attractive but rotten-at-heart Earl (Robert Ryan), it used the love between the young couple, Peggy and Joe, as a contrast to emphasize the steamy melodrama of the triangle.

Not that Monroe played her part with dewy innocence; sexiness was still the mainspring of her performance, as *Variety* noticed, saying that she managed to get it over well in one or two scenes. When the film reached England, the London *Daily Express* said that 'that strident young blonde Marilyn Monroe showed a jagged

quality that made the rocks along the sea coast gentle'. Whatever they meant by this strange comment, it hardly squared with Alton Cook's comment in the *New York World Telegram and Sun* that 'this girl has a refreshing exuberance, and an abundance of girlish high spirits'. Mr. Cook considered her to be a forceful actress, too, a view echoed by Irene Thirer in the *New York Post*, who said that Marilyn Monroe was a real acting threat to current screen blondes.

All in all, not a bad crop of reviews, but Fox, who had loaned her out to R.K.O. at a fairly modest fee for *Clash by Night*, brought her quickly back into the fold to make yet another light-as-air comedy, *We're Not Married*, rather than offering her anything as juicy as *Clash by Night*.

It was about this time (May 1952) that David Lewin, a British film journalist and commentator on the lives of film stars,

To help attract publicity for Clash by Night, *Monroe and Keith Andes managed some exuberant beach exercises for the stills cameraman.*

The crowd's vote clearly going to gorgeous married – or is she unmarried? – mother Marilyn Monroe in a bathing beauty contest in We're Not Married *(1952).*

asked in the *Daily Express* where in the Hollywood tradition did Miss Monroe fit. 'Her name is not yet familiar in England, though in twelve months her film rating has risen faster than the cost of living.' Dubious about her acting talents, Lewin concluded 'Maybe Miss Monroe's safest bet would be to stay as a pin-up.'

It was probably this sort of doubt lingering in the minds of the powers-that-be at Twentieth Century-Fox that was responsible for Marilyn spending much of 1952 working in films that with one exception had no dramatic pretensions at all.

Not that there was anything wrong with *We're Not Married*, described by the *Daily Express* as a 'wry and often funny omnibus film', for it was, in fact, a thoroughly entertaining movie. The film concerned the problems that arose for five married couples who discovered they were not legally married after all, and treated each of the couple's stories quite separately. Some very good actors feat-

ured on the lengthy cast list, though their talents were perhaps a little dissipated by the fact that they never got together. Marilyn probably never even saw on set Louis Calhern or Paul Douglas, with whom she had recently worked and who were both in the film.

The problems given the five couples – Ginger Rogers and Fred Allen, Marilyn Monroe and David Wayne, Eve Arden and Paul Douglas, Eddie Bracken and Mitzi Gaynor, and Louis Calhern and Zsa Zsa Gabor – were caused by the fact that the Justice of the Peace, who had married them all two and a half years before, suddenly discovered that his licence to perform marriage ceremonies did not actually become valid until a few days later. A flurry of Western Union telegrams alerted the couples to their suddenly sinful state.

Nunnally Johnson, one of Hollywood's most respected writers, whose long list of screenplays already included such fine films as *The Grapes of Wrath*, *Tobacco*

Road, *The Gunfighter, The Desert Fox* and *Phone Call From a Stranger* and who was to write and produce one of Monroe's most successful films, *How to Marry a Millionaire*, was screenwriter and producer of this one. His screenplay looked at the institution of marriage from several viewpoints and ensured that director Edmund Goulding, well-known for his sympathetic directing of female stars, had a good basis on which to work. Even so, Goulding did not seem able to get a great deal out of Marilyn Monroe. She looked beautiful, but seemed unable to project any real emotion.

She played a young housewife, Annabel, married to Jeff Norris (David Wayne). They have a small son, rising two, and a pretty house, but Annabel is restless and goes in for beauty contests, to her husband's disapproval. Apart from the fact that he is the one left wearing an apron in the kitchen, he happens to believe that a woman's place is in the home and so, when she had just won the 'Mrs. Mississippi' contest and is planning to go on to the 'Mrs. America' contest he is quite happy to learn that he and Annabel are not married. No go, says Jeff, you are not 'Mrs.' anything. Annabel thinks about

A girl does not get out of feeding her son just because she has been crowned 'Mrs. Mississippi': Marilyn giving cereal to an unenthusiastic baby while disgruntled and aproned husband David Wayne looks on in a scene from We're Not Married.

this while feeding the baby (still wearing her 'Mrs. Mississippi' crown and ermine-trimmed robe). Well, she reasons, if she is not married, she can quite legally go in for the 'Miss Mississippi' contest, and does so, with resigned husband and small son in the audience to see her win. Later, again with son to watch the proceedings, they get married again, this time legally.

The story was pretty light stuff, to be sure, and perhaps Marilyn found it difficult to work up any enthusiasm about being married to David Wayne, a nice guy, but not exactly exciting. On the other hand, she had herself once been married to a good man who had tried to suppress her own ambitions in that line, and might have been expected to be able to contribute some genuine feeling to the part.

Two directors, Huston in *The Asphalt Jungle* and Mankiewicz in *All About Eve* had coaxed fine performances out of her. It remained to be seen if she could coax them out of herself.

Queen of all she surveys: Monroe as the beauty contest winning mother in We're Not Married.

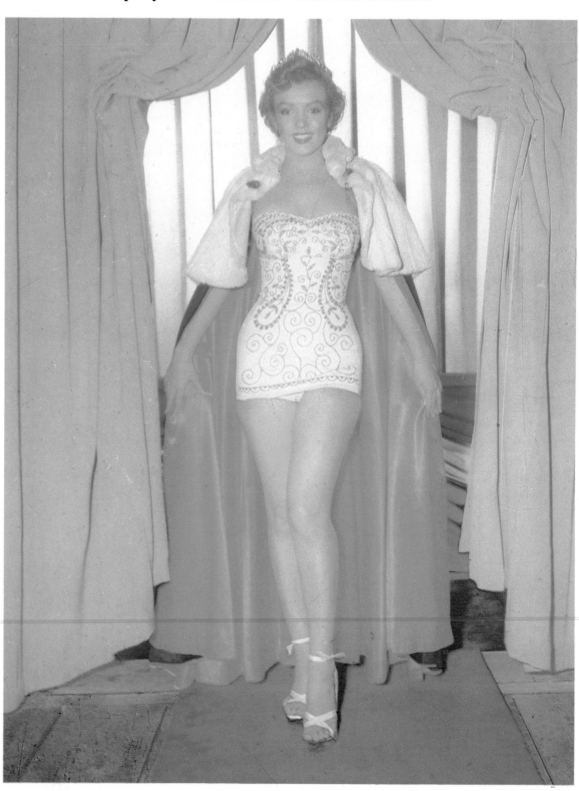

'I Just Want To Be Wonderful'

Journalist Pete Martin, in his slight but perceptive book about Marilyn (*Marilyn Monroe*, written in the mid-1950s), recounted a story told him by a man working in the legal department at Twentieth Century-Fox. The man had pointed out to Monroe that if she signed the contract she was negotiating in the current financial year rather than the next, she would save herself quite a bit of money. Monroe had looked at him and said 'I am not interested in money. I just want to be wonderful.' Then she had left, apparently without signing the contract.

It was such an extraordinary thing for her to have said, and so unexpected that it rivets one's attention. Not the bit about the money: Monroe never seems to have been particularly concerned about money or even to have understood how to handle it; nor was she concerned either about how she spent it, or about how much she actually had at any given moment. It is true that she had more than one argument with Fox about her contractual salary which, as she grew more and more of a money-spinner for the studio, began to look ludicrously small compared with what other Twentieth Century-Fox stars were earning. Such arguments were about a matter of principle, however, rather than numbers of dollars. It may be true, too, as some have said, that Monroe was mean about small things like the cost of her train journeys or about giving presents to studio people working on her films. This, if it were true, probably stemmed from the 'training' her character had received in childhood, when tiny sums like a dime or a quarter had to be divided up into even smaller sums to go into the church collection plate.

It is the word 'wonderful' that is surprising. If she had said 'famous' or 'the greatest film star in the world' or just, like Muhammed Ali, 'the greatest', we could understand the motivation easily enough, because the drive for success is a well-understood human condition. To want to be wonderful is a quite different ambition. 'Wonderful' in terms of what? Beauty of person, perhaps: wonderful as a work of art. Or wonderful in terms of acting ability: a wonder of the age, like Sarah Siddons or Sarah Bernhardt, perhaps.

The thing about being 'wonderful', in fact, is that your ambitions can remain amorphous, ambiguous. If you are unsure of your acting abilities, then you

Marilyn in pensive mood – perhaps induced by the title of the book she has apparently been reading.

don't have to be wonderful in those terms: if you know that your hair colour, your very name is not the real you, then you can think in terms of being wonderful through the projection of a personality that will still surely shine through somehow, no matter how deep it has been buried under the public persona you and hundreds of busy people are creating for you. You can be wonderful simply by existing.

Being 'wonderful' suggests that you are so special, so excellent, delightful, ex-

tremely good or fine, marvellous, extraordinary and remarkable, to quote the dictionary definitions, that people will look upon you with admiration and love, emotions that are not necessarily aroused by simple fame.

Because Marilyn wanted to be thought wonderful by everybody, by the whole world, she could not just exist. She had to bring herself to the world's notice. And since she had been taught since childhood that being a film star was a wholly

Marilyn in love with life. The camera catches the fleeting moment as the effervescent beauty reaches for the sky.

desirable state, that was the way in which she would achieve the world's notice. She could not conceive of any other.

Which was perhaps the whole problem. She had chosen to become wonderful through a profession that she was never totally confident she could practise successfully. Hence the insistence on the drama coach on set, the attendance at all those drama classes where she was a watcher rather than a performer, the chronic lateness both at work and in her private life, the later inability to remember or say the simplest line and, of course, all the drugs and drink.

Since this is an awful lot of theory to hang on one word, perhaps one should turn to the practical and see just how the blossoming film career was making out. How wonderful was Marilyn?

Well, in 1952, not very, not as a movie actress anyway. Twentieth Century-Fox were putting her mostly into parts that showed off the shapely figure and the sex appeal and in which acting ability was not all that important. They seemed to be hedging their bets even about the sex appeal, for they never gave her a part in which she achieved the result the exhibiting of sex appeal was supposed to achieve – catching an attractive man. She was nearly always the girl in whom men might take a passing sexual interest but whom they did not want on any more permanent basis. In *We're Not Married* she had been given a husband whose sex appeal and general good looks were not all that obvious: nice guy, David Wayne, but not the sort of man one would expect the gorgeous Marilyn to be interested in.

Marilyn in full war paint, hair newly tinted and set, sparkles at the 1952 Photoplay Awards Dinner. Behind her are Hollywood stalwarts Alan Ladd and Dick Powell.

Twentieth Century-Fox gave Monroe one dramatic role that required acting ability rather than sex appeal in 1952. This was in *Don't Bother to Knock*, in which she starred with that fine and dependable actor, Richard Widmark, and with Anne Bancroft, making her movie debut.

The film had originally been announced as *Night without Sleep*, which might have been a better title than *Don't Bother to Knock*, with its suggestion of dropped trousers and bedroom farce, for the film was very definitely not a comedy. In it, Marilyn played a babysitter who tried to kill her charge. She was not even allowed to look particularly attractive in the film.

The action of *Don't Bother to Knock* takes place in the course of one evening in a New York hotel. Richard Widmark is Jed Towers, an airline pilot whose outward tough-guy manner hides a caring, compassionate nature. He has come to stay in the hotel because his girlfriend Lyn Leslie (Anne Bancroft) is singing in cabaret there. Also booked in at the hotel are a couple, Ruth and Peter Jones (Lurenne Tuttle and Jim Backus) who have gone out on the town, leaving their small daughter Bunny (Donna Corcoran) in the care of a babysitter, Nell (Monroe), found for them by the hotel's elevator attendant Eddie (Elisha Cook Jr.).

Nell is, in fact, Eddie's niece. She is also a girl whose mental balance has been upset by the loss of her fiancé who had been killed in a wartime plane crash, though Nell's mind is not yet prepared to accept the fact.

Jed arrives at the hotel only to be given the brush-off by Lyn who has decided that she does not care for his apparently hard, uncaring nature. Thoroughly disgruntled, he takes himself off to his room thinking 'to hell with all women', or words to that effect. This view of the sex changes abruptly when he notices through a window on the other side of the hotel an attractive young blonde trying on a lacy black negligee (Mrs. Jones's).

Soon, Jed has insinuated himself into the Jones's suite, into Nell's good graces and, before too long, into her arms as well.

The two are just settling down for a pleasant evening when Bunny awakes and walks in on them. Nell, enraged, sends her back to her room so harshly that the child bursts into tears. It quickly transpires that Nell's mad rage was triggered off by the fact that she thought Bunny was interrupting a glad reunion between her and her lost fiancé: in her psychotic state she has decided that Jed is her fiancé.

Jed realizes that she is mentally unbalanced but before he can talk quietly with her, and perhaps disabuse her mind of its sad mistake about him, there is another knock on the door. Nell insists Jed hide in the bathroom before she answers the knock, which turns out to be Uncle Eddie. Already keyed up, Nell is even more disturbed when her uncle unfortunately mentions her fiancé, and she hits out at him with a heavy ashtray. Luckily, he is not hurt badly.

Finally, Jed leaves the room, thinking that Eddie will be able to control Nell and look after Bunny. But Eddie, too, leaves and Nell, alone with Bunny, decides that it was the little girl's fault that Jed walked out, and ties her up, preparatory to killing her.

Opposite: *The wide blue eyes are wistfully innocent, the mouth, despite the heavy lipstick, is soft and tender. Combined with the sophisticated hairstyle and glittering jewellery, the effect is uniquely, miraculously Marilyn.*

Below: *The dowdy babysitter has just knocked her uncle out cold – Marilyn varying her sex star image with a dramatic role in* Don't Bother to Knock *(1952). Tending the wounded Elisha Cook Jr. is Richard Widmark.*

Alerted to trouble by some sixth sense, Jed rushes back to the Jones's suite to find Nell struggling with Bunny's mother and manages to separate them, though he cannot prevent Nell fleeing from the room. When he finds her she has attacked a third person and is now sitting in the hotel lobby with a razor in her hand, ready to kill herself. Among the small crowd gathered around her is Lyn, trying to persuade her to give up the razor. When she sees Jed, Nell quietly gives him the weapon. The police come and take her away – not to prison, Jed explains, but to hospital where she will be made better again. As she leaves she acknowledges that she now accepts that her fiancé is dead.

A dramatic and sombre story, indeed, and a quite startling change of style for Marilyn. It was, perhaps, too startling. Many film goers and critics considered it to be a waste of her more obvious talents, while the part did not allow her to indicate whether she had any real acting talent or not.

It is possible that it was the film's director rather than the part that did not give her room to manoeuvre. Roy Baker, an Englishman who gained much of his early film-making experience in the British cinema's very fine documentary tradition, was perhaps not imaginative enough in his handling of the story or of its female lead to bring out the best in either. Mindful of a tight budget, he chose to rehearse the action carefully in advance, and then shoot the story straight through, allowing very few retakes.

Marilyn, having rehearsed the part in detail with Natasha Lytess, apparently worked out an interpretation that called upon Nell to behave most of the time in a slightly dazed, unresponsive style, with sudden, frightening explosions of hysteria being triggered off by external causes. Baker's way of working meant that she had to get her interpretation of every scene right first time, and could not feel her way into it.

The result, for many professional critics, was a wooden performance that failed to project anything very much. They did not, on the whole, think she was very good, but neither did they think she was very bad. Some were irritatingly condescending, sounding pleased with themselves that they were saying something

nice about the little blonde with the pneumatic curves.

On the whole, the trade papers were the kindest. *Variety*, while relegating the film to the 'support-booking only' slot, said that Marilyn Monroe gave an excellent account of herself in a strictly dramatic role that commanded a certain attention. The British trade paper *Kinematograph Weekly* (admittedly a decidedly parochial publication) said that Marilyn Monroe gave a particularly moving and subtle performance. While reminding his readers that she was more renowned for her striking frontal development, the reviewer went on to say that she gave the film a tender touch without taking the edge off the essential tension. Like *Variety*'s man, he thought the film was double-bill stuff.

Above: The lady and the tramp – except that the lady turned out to be a streetwalker. Marilyn Monroe and Charles Laughton in the delightful 'The Cop and the Anthem' sequence from O. Henry's Full House (1952).

Opposite: More fur-trimmed elegance, with smooth sophistication the key note of this glamour portrait of c. 1950.

After this, Marilyn went back to the lighter side of Hollywood for her last two films to be released during 1952. First came an omnibus of tales by that master of the short story, O. Henry. Given the nicely poker-ish title of *O. Henry's Full House,* the film contained five short stories, each with its own cast, director and scriptwriter.

Monroe was in the story generally thought by the critics to be the most memorable, largely because of Charles Laughton's wonderful, warm and comic playing of a bum called Soapy. This was 'The Cop and the Anthem', directed by Henry Koster, and the first story in the film.

Below: *Poster for* Monkey Business *(1952).*

The nip of winter is in the air as the story opens, and Soapy and fellow down-and-out Horace (David Wayne) are discussing how best to cope with the on-coming bad weather. Soapy decides he is going to get himself taken into prison for some not-too-serious crime that will just allow him a couple of warm months off the streets. Adjusting his bowler hat and setting his flower at exactly the right angle in his buttonhole, for Soapy is a fastidiously elegant bum, right down to his spats, he sets off looking for a nice little crime to commit.

He has had no luck at all when he sees a glorious vision in the street ahead of him. It is a woman, but what a woman. Clad from neck to ankle in a dress of form-fitting Prince of Wales check, her blonde head topped by a cheeky little hat, and with her hands thrust into a fur muff, she is indeed a beautiful creature. Even better, from Soapy's point of view, there is a cop in the vicinity. Reasoning that if he accosts the lady, perfectly politely of course, she will scream for the policeman who will arrest him, Soapy picks up speed and catches up with the lady outside a carpet shop. To his embarrassed horror, he discovers that she is a streetwalker and flees.

Later, he and Horace are sitting in the warmth of a church, where the atmosphere makes Soapy start reflecting on the evils of his life. Lost in thoughts of reforming himself and even getting a job, Soapy fails to notice the policeman who walks into the church. Horace does and flees, leaving Soapy to be arrested on a vagrancy charge.

Archer Winsten in the *New York Post* described Monroe in 'The Cop and the Anthem' as a 'streetwalker of stunning proportions'. He might well: her bosom makes one think of brassière advertisements. If there is just a thought that perhaps it is not all Monroe, it's as well to remember her oft-quoted reply to the same accusation: 'Those who know me better, know better.'

There were several fine actors with Monroe in the film that wound up her list for 1952. This was *Monkey Business,* starring Cary Grant, Ginger Rogers and Charles Coburn as well as Marilyn Monroe, and directed by Howard Hawks. One of Hollywood's all-time greats among

CARY GINGER CHARLES MARILYN
GRANT • ROGERS • COBURN • MONROE

IN HOWARD HAWKS'

"monkey business"

20th CENTURY FOX

Produced by SOL C. SIEGEL • Directed by HOWARD HAWKS • Story by HARRY SEGALL • Screen Play by BEN HECHT, CHARLES LEDERER and I. A. L. DIAMOND

directors, Hawks had already directed Grant in three vintage comedies, *Bringing Up Baby*, *His Girl Friday* and *I was A Male War Bride*, and doubtless hoped that this would be another.

It didn't quite come off, partly because the story, being neither screwball nor sophisticated like the other three, was more plain silly than good farce. Three writers had a hand in the script, Ben Hecht, I.A.L. Diamond and Charles Lederer, which perhaps accounts for the rather bumpy way the story moves along.

In *Monkey Business* Cary Grant plays Barnaby Fulton, a research biochemist working in a large factory owned by a Mr. Oxley (Charles Coburn). At home, Barnaby has an attractive and loving wife, Edwina (Ginger Rogers); in his laboratory at Mr. Oxley's factory Barnaby has installed, for experimental purposes, a chimpanzee called Esther. Mr. Oxley has

installed in his office a beautiful platinum blonde secretary, Lois Laurel (Monroe), who signals her role by walking about with a notebook and sharp pencil in her hand. She is presumably there to give the aging Mr. Oxley visual pleasure, since as a secretary she can hardly stick a stamp straight on a letter. Basic secretarial skills like spelling, punctuation, shorthand and typing are all equally beyond her.

Thus the *dramatis personae*, except that Esther turns out to be more of a *dea ex machina*, single-handedly changing the course of the lives of all concerned, if only temporarily, when she escapes from her cage one day and tips a random mixture of chemicals into the open water cooler used by the laboratory staff.

Barnaby's recent experiments have been concerned with finding a formula for a drug that will restore a youthful zest for life in human beings past their first youth.

Ginger Rogers, Charles Coburn and Marilyn Monroe in earnest discussion about the Monkey Business *going on in Coburn's laboratory.*

Being a responsible sort of man, he experiments on himself as well as on monkeys. Shortly after Esther has done her own piece of laboratory practical work, Barnaby decides to taste his latest formula, washing it down with water from the cooler. Very soon he is frisking about like a jiving teenager, swanning out of the laboratory as if he hasn't a care in the world.

Mr. Oxley, concerned, sends Miss Laurel to look for him and bring him back to work. Barnaby, still acting under the influence, scoops Miss Laurel up and takes her off on a spree during which they indulge in all sorts of things he has not thought about for years – driving a fast car, roller-skating, swimming. Miss Laurel loves the drive in the open-top sports car and looks fetching indeed in a well-fitting, low-cut hired swimsuit such as was never seen, before or since, on a peg in any public swimming pool costumes-for-hire collection.

Eventually, the effect of the chemical mix wears off and Barnaby returns to normal. Unfortunately, his wife Edwina, visiting his laboratory, also tries out the formula, also washing it down with water from the cooler. . . . Her particular reaction is a shocking desire to be taken off by her husband for a re-play of their honeymoon.

There is quite a lot more of this sort of thing, even involving Mr. Oxley and his entire board of directors; during the course of their shenanigans, Miss Laurel gets squirted with soda water and ends up having to box the ears of both Mr. Oxley and Barnaby.

No film with the witty, debonair and amusing Cary Grant and the attractive Ginger Rogers in the lead parts could be entirely without merit, though the two, were, as the English popular newspaper, the *Star*, put it, skimming over thin ice in diving boots for much of *Monkey Business*. The paper's reviewer was made to

A helping hand or two from Marilyn for a drug-crazed Cary Grant, unable to control his roller skates in Monkey Business.

85

The image turns from all-American to sophisticated Continental as Marilyn displays saucy camiknickers for this 1953 pose.

feel very old indeed by their embarrassing teenage and tinytot antics, so much so that Marilyn Monroe's secretary apparently shimmied past him almost unnoticed: he named her but had nothing to say about her performance.

On the whole, she was noticed for her shape and her walk. Whether moving towards the camera or away from it, her appearance provoked whistles and other positive responses from audiences and critics alike. 'Suggestive' was the word for her performance; acting had nothing to do with it.

In truth, she was rather wooden, and her voice was not good. As in *Don't Bother to Knock*, she was apt to become shrill when she had to express any emotion.

Perhaps it was nerves and tiredness. Five films starring Marilyn Monroe were released during the course of 1952. Since she put in a lot of work in her own time on her roles, she could hardly have allowed herself a break from the hot-house world of film-making for months.

To be fair, also, Marilyn had worked on much of *Monkey Business* with a rumbling appendix, made quiescent by drugs. She could not have felt anything like on top form.

She knew very well that however indifferent her films were, however unremarkable her own performances were in them, the eyes of America were on her. Everywhere her name was in lights above cinemas and bringing in the audiences in droves; box-office returns were excellent. Her name and stories about her cropped up constantly in newspapers and magazines; the first major profile about Marilyn Monroe, woman and film star, had been published in the respectable *Colliers* magazine months before. She was big news, a hot property and she knew it. All the more reason, then, to be good, to be wonderful.

It was quite a burden for a girl on her own to carry. What was clear, though, was that she had been more wooden, less relaxed in her films after Natasha Lytess appeared on set than she had been before. Was it that yet another pair of eyes coolly analyzing her performances had caused her nerves to tighten in her throat so that her voice came out as a squeak, and in her body so that her limbs refused to move easily? The paralyzing effects of nervous-

ness are not uncommon among public performers, and Marilyn by now was public property.

If Marilyn Monroe the film star was public property, Monroe the woman was still able to keep herself to herself. For much of 1952 her home base was a suite decorated to her own specifications in the splendidly expensive Bel-Air Hotel. She had tried a house and apartments of her own, but had not liked them. Perhaps she wanted to be by herself but with the feeling that she was surrounded by other people, a feeling a hotel could convey very well. She was always to like good hotels, perhaps because of their atmosphere of calm, quiet wealth.

During the filming of *Monkey Business* she met a man who was to change the course of her surprisingly solitary life. It was a blind date, and she had to be persuaded to go, thinking that she could hardly have anything in common with a

The world's press cut Cary Grant out of this off-set picture of Marilyn Monroe and Joe DiMaggio during the filming of Monkey Business *so that he could not spoil the romantic atmosphere.*

ball-player. She knew nothing about baseball and who was this Joe DiMaggio, anyway? The name rang a bell, but that was about all.

The evening, arranged by a mutual friend, started out as a typical Marilyn Monroe Film Star affair. She turned up hours late for a start, and chose to come dressed up to suit the image in a very well fitting two-piece and full war paint. Then she reverted to little Norma Jean and hardly said a word all evening. Neither did Joe, a quiet man anyway.

Eleven years older than Marilyn, Joe DiMaggio was an American gentleman. He was quietly spoken, quietly and well dressed, and preferred a simple life. His evenings were spent watching television in a family atmosphere or playing cards with his men friends – he moved through life with his good-looking head high above the crowd. His brilliant baseball career, which had made him an American folk hero, was now confined to exhibition matches and although he was more of a businessman and a restaurant owner than a sportsman Joe DiMaggio was still very much a man to be reckoned with.

Marilyn was not immediately impressed, but soon she found herself thinking about him quite a lot. It was not long before their friendship had become the talk of America. They were photographed together with Cary Grant on the set of *Monkey Business*, but the press were not going to let Cary Grant come between them and a good story and cut him out. Marilyn was asked if she and Joe were engaged; came the stock reply: 'We are just good friends.' She was asked if they had been discussing love. 'Love is not something you *discuss*' she replied, though she might perhaps have said that she and Joe did not really discuss anything very much. Joe was a man who did things rather than talk about them.

All too soon, Joe flew back east while Marilyn finished off *Monkey Business*, had her appendix removed and did a piece of public relations that soon became part of the mythology of Monroe, the girl with the genius for one-line cracks. Were her remarks the work of a girl with a needle-witted brain beneath the platinum, or were they dreamed up by publicity men feeding her the results of their clever thinking over steaming typewriters?

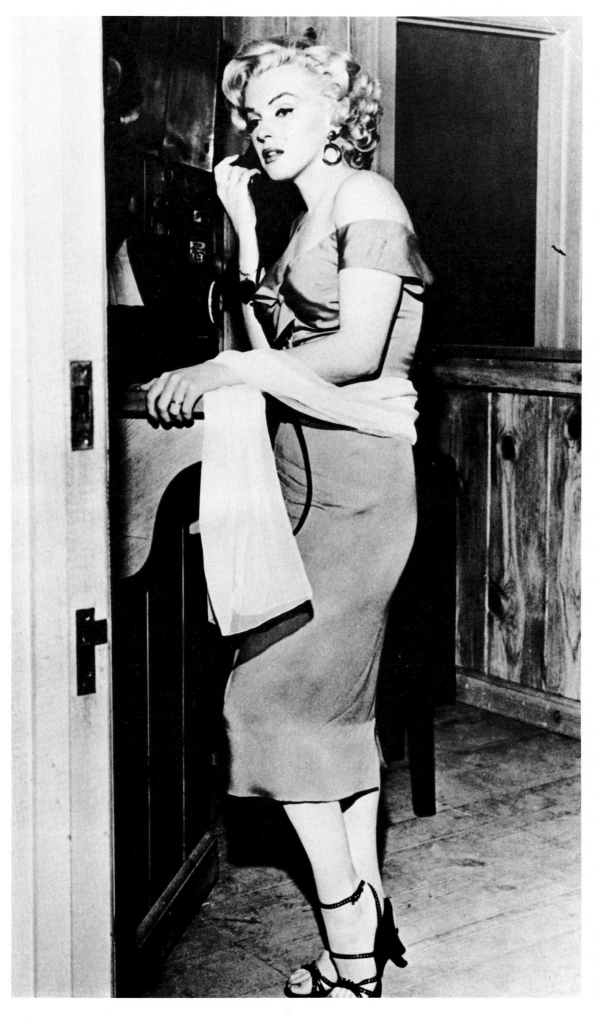

Opposite: *A polka-dot scarf seems to be all that is covering the Monroe essentials, which is no doubt the effect photographer Frank Powolny was after in this pin-up shot.*

Left: *The dress cut 'so low it shows her knees' does not inhibit Monroe's telephoning abilities in Niagara (1953).*

Nobody has ever been quite sure, and there is nothing that helps a myth along like a bit of obscurity.

The occasion for the myth-making was a Marine training camp, Pendleton, where she made a personal appearance for the benefit of the 10,000 or so men stationed there. She sang them some songs, danced a bit, and captivated them. They would not let her finish. The air was full of screams and wolf whistles as they clamoured for more. She was wonderful, they all loved her. These were the sort of men who had recently voted her 'The Girl we'd most like to climb a hill with'; and in the Aleutians 'The Girl most likely to thaw out Alaska.' In Korea, the vote of M.A.S.H. personnel had been 'The Girl we would most like to examine'. Looking out over the sea of faces, relaxed, free of nerves, she laughed and said she could not understand why boys like them were always getting so excited over sweater girls. 'Take away their sweaters and what have they got?' she asked reasonably. As a remark redolent of come-hither sex appeal, it was more successful even than her innocent 'Only the radio' had been when she was asked whether she had had anything on at all while being photographed for 'Golden Dreams'.

There was to be nothing innocent about the sex in Marilyn's next film *Niagara*, a tense tale of murder and counter-murder set against the stunning background of the Falls. This was to be Marilyn's biggest opportunity to show her dramatic ability, and she grasped it with both hands.

Henry Hathaway, who had been making films with skill and an easy competence since the early 1930s, was to direct, and he had many discussions with Marilyn about her part before the cameras rolled. As there were several weeks of location shooting at Niagara in up-state New York, Marilyn managed to grab the opportunity to spend a few days in New York City with Joe DiMaggio. It was not entirely successful with, on the one hand, so many Easterners demanding interviews with her, and on the other a whole posse of newspapermen following her every public action with Joe. He talked about marriage, but she stalled. In the end she went back to finish *Niagara* with nothing resolved.

In *Niagara* Marilyn plays Rose Loomis, a beautiful and sexy young mar-

ried woman given to wearing dresses cut so low 'you can see her knees'. Her husband George (Joseph Cotten) seems from the outset a strange, moody man. He also has an odd-ball view of his wife's attractions. Trying to explain how he had come to love her, a bar waitress, he said he guessed he liked the way 'she put the beer on the table'.

The couple are watched by another young couple Polly and Ray Cutler (Jean Peters and Casey Adams) staying at the same motel in that honeymooners' paradise, Niagara. It is through their eyes that the audience sees the early part of the story. It seems at first that it is George who may be trying to murder his wife, but

Above: *Marilyn shows off the famous magenta red dress she wore in* Niagara *and which upset so many of the good women of America.*

Opposite: *Monroe and her soon-to-be-killed boyfriend Richard Allen kiss in the mists made by the Falls in* Niagara.

Polly comes across the beautiful Rose kissing another man; and she is clearly in love with him rather than her husband. It becomes apparent that it is Rose who is trying to dispose of her husband and that she is persuading her lover Patrick (Richard Allen) to do the dirty deed.

When Loomis disappears and Rose is called upon to identify what may be his body, she collapses and has to be put under sedation in hospital. The body is Patrick's. Loomis eventually re-appears, unshaven and haggard, before a terrified Polly who thinks he is going to kill her. In fact, he has killed Patrick, but in self-defence, he explains, and now just wants to get away and forget Rose and everything to do with her.

Rose, terrified that Loomis is pursuing her, checks herself out of the hospital and tries to go into hiding. But Loomis catches up with her, pursuing her up the famous Niagara landmark, the Carillon Tower, where he strangles her. Fleeing from the scene of the crime, Loomis commandeers a boat to which Polly had returned to collect food for a picnic. Together, they are whirled down the river towards the Falls and seemingly inevitable death. Loomis manages to push Polly on to a ledge, from which she is rescued by a helicopter, while he plunges to his doom.

Marilyn looked stunningly beautiful in *Niagara*, and gave a convincing performance in what was a pretty torrid tale.

It was meant to catch public attention, to be a huge box office draw, and it was. Since it was successful in financial terms, and since audiences went to it in droves, it perhaps does not matter that the critics were not unanimous in their praise.

American reviews of *Niagara* were on the whole favourable as far as Marilyn was concerned, though they had a few reservations about the worthiness of the story line, and were still not 100 per cent sure about her abilities as an actress. There were no reservations about her looks and shape. She was, said *Time* magazine, 'what lifts the film above the commonplace.'

Over the other side of the Atlantic, British critics said much the same thing, but what they meant was her presence in this silly film may have lifted it out of the ordinary, but only to drop it into the pretty dreadful.

The august *Times* newspaper said that *Niagara* was 'one of the silliest films seen in the cinema for some time. Miss Monroe, teetering about in ridiculous clothes, seems, understandably perhaps, set on self-parody.'

The *Daily Mail* was sarcastic: 'Although she has been seen before in various pictures', said the paper's reviewer dismissively, '*Niagara* is the one chosen to confound us with the high mature glory of the finished product. The reports seem to have been slightly exaggerated. Miss Monroe is a little blonde cutie with a three-dimensional body and a half-dimensional talent.'

Donald Zec shared his views with the millions of readers of the *Daily Mirror*. He had, of course, noticed the red dress, suggesting Marilyn had to unzip to breathe. He was not convinced about her acting, and he did not like her voice which he considered to be 'high, thin and nasal, despite that prima-donna bosom and comfy diaphragm'. Nor was he impressed by her singing: 'Her song "Kiss" should keep her out of musicals permanently.'

'Kiss' had, in fact, been a cause of particular agitation among a certain section of American womanhood. According to *Variety*, many women's groups had written to Twentieth Century-Fox complaining that *Niagara* and 'Kiss' would have a bad effect on their sweethearts, husbands and children. Since such reactions are a publicity department's dream, Fox were no doubt delighted. Maybe they had themselves leaked the story to *Variety*, and from there it was picked up by the world's newspapers.

About the most perceptive of the English newspaper reviews of Marilyn in *Niagara*, though he thought the film 'a rough crossing', came from Gavin Lambert in the *Evening Standard*. 'This well-formed but rather mysterious girl, affectionately photographed in shower bath and shift, humming "Thrill me, thrill me, thrill me" in an offhand kind of way, does not fit into any of the cinema's established categories of blondes,' observed Mr. Lambert.

'Her acting can best be described as reluctant. She is too passive to be a vamp; she is no menace because so easily frightened, and she is certainly not a bombshell, for she never bursts.

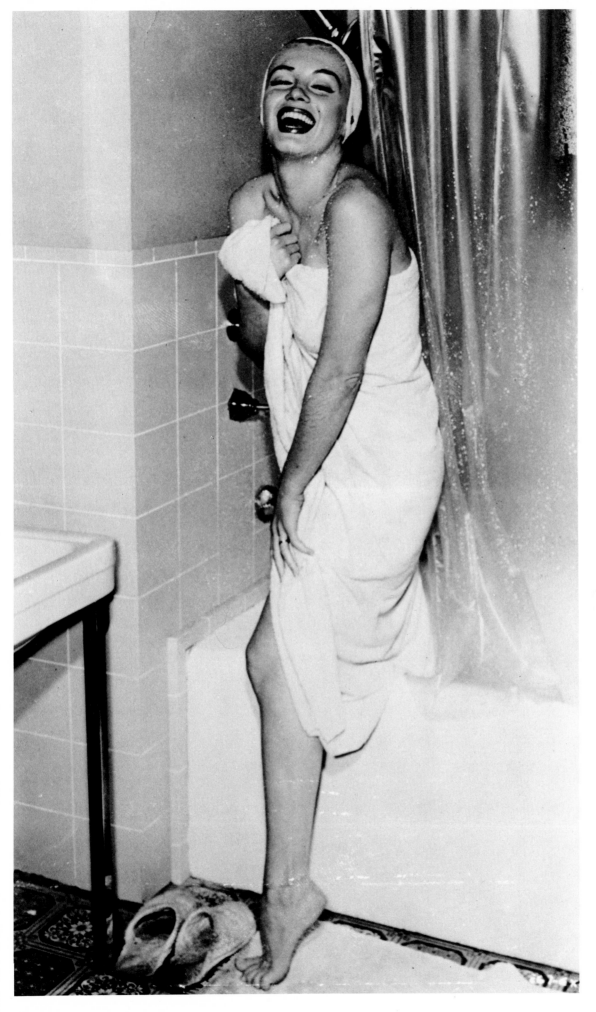

Surely the inelegant
slippers on the floor do
not belong to the lovely
lady stepping out of her
shower in the honeymoon
bungalow at Niagara?

'She walks – only this can account for the enormous swaying of her hips – as if the whole earth were a tightrope on which she has to balance. Her face, with its eyes inclined to pop and mouth perpetually parted for a kiss, looks vaguely drugged. For all the wolf calls . . . there is something oddly mournful about Miss Monroe. She doesn't look happy. She lacks the pin-up's cheerful grin.'

Well, maybe, but Twentieth Century-Fox were grinning, all the way to the bank. Their famous reluctant actress was pulling in millions of dollars for them, even in Britain, despite, or perhaps because of, the reviews. British cinema audiences have never been known for their slavish attention to what the critics say, and the mere fact that they chose to notice Marilyn with such a deluge of words and reviews suggested that here was someone a bit special, good actress or not.

There was to be a six-month gap before Fox released their next Monroe film. This was *Gentlemen Prefer Blondes*, a Broadway smash which Fox had bought for a huge sum as a big film for Betty Grable. But Betty Grable's sun was setting and Fox decided that they could not risk trying to recoup their stakes using her, especially as it was going to cost them another huge sum to produce the film in the lavish style they had in mind. Instead, they gave the part of Lorelei Lee as played with enormous éclat on Broadway by Carol Channing, to Marilyn Monroe. It was not that much of a gamble, since simply putting her name at the head of the cast list was enough to ensure big audiences, but they made doubly sure by bringing in that other very sexy lady, Jane Russell, to play the brunette, Dorothy. To get Howard Hughes, to whom Russell was contracted, to release her, Fox had to agree to give her top billing.

A lot of effort went into *Gentlemen Prefer Blondes* from all concerned, and it made Fox a great deal of money, but general critical reception at the time was low key, and it is probably much more admired now than it was then. Maybe the critics of the day were too close to the film's two stars and their 'love goddesses' image to believe that their performances had any real artistic integrity.

Hollis Alpert, critic of the *Saturday Review*, considered the film 'an empty and graceless remake . . . that only comes alive when Marilyn Monroe and Jane Russell stop talking and start wiggling', a view partly shared by Mr. Beverley Baxter, British Member of Parliament and journalist who was given plenty of space in the *Evening Standard* to be offensively rude to the film and, by implication, to his own parliamentary constituents: 'I predict an enormous success for this picture. It is dull, stupid and boring beyond words. It is an insult to human intelligence. Therefore we can be certain that wherever this picture is shown there will be an eager capacity audience.'

At least Mr. Alpert was sufficiently beguiled by Marilyn's attractions to have to admit that although he had 'made an honest attempt to evaluate her singing, dancing and acting ability . . . I couldn't keep my mind on the problem.' Not so Mr. Baxter. 'The poor little creature limps through a plot which keeps on dying . . . .' Time has proved them wrong; probably most people knew even then that they were wrong. Today, *Gentlemen Prefer Blondes* looks a highly entertaining, amusing musical, a classic typical of its age. Marilyn's presence in it is light, delicious, magical, stupendously sexy; she displays a neat sense of comedy, and her inimitable, soft-voiced singing makes her songs utterly unforgettable. From this distance, we can see easily that her dippy, dumb blonde Lorelei is a performance from a true professional, a piece of role playing, and not just Monroe being herself in black net tights and sequins.

Gentlemen Prefer Blondes, based on the stories and aphorisms of Anita Loos, who wrote the Broadway musical comedy with Joseph Fields, traces the adventures of two night-club entertainers on their way to Paris in search of romance and, in Lorelei's case, money.

Lorelei has the money well in sight, in fact. It belongs to Gus Esmond (Tommy Noonan) a mild, bespectacled young man to whom she has managed to engage herself, despite his father's belief that she is only in it for the money. In an effort to prise Tommy away from Lorelei, Esmond Sr. hires a private detective, Malone (Elliot Reid), to pursue the two ladies to Paris and bring back evidence of Lorelei's bad faith.

While on board the ship taking them to France, Dorothy falls in love with Malone – much to Lorelei's exasperation, who feels that Dorothy ought to be doing better for herself, dollar-wise. Metaphorically sticking pins in the passenger list, Lorelei comes up with Henry Spofford III, wealthy and a better catch for Dorothy. Henry Spofford III turns out to be about ten years old. Nothing daunted, Lorelei then turns her attention to ageing diamond-merchant Sir Francis Beekman (Charles Coburn), purely for sociable reasons, as Sir Francis is already married. It is all very innocent, but looks bad when seen from a distance through the eyes and camera lens of the private detective Malone.

When they arrive in Paris the girls find that Gus, alerted by Dad to Lorelei's apparent perfidy, has withdrawn their credit rating, so they have to find work as night-club entertainers. There are a few more complications, involving Sir Francis, a stolen tiara and a court case before all ends happily, with Lorelei reconciled to Gus and to her future father-in-law, and Dorothy spliced to Malone.

Marilyn Monroe and Jane Russell turned out to be a memorable duo, working wonderfully well together, both in their musical routines and in the general action of the film. Together they sang the Jule Styne and Leo Robin number 'Two Little Girls from Little Rock' and 'When Love Goes Wrong' by Hoagy Carmichael and Harold Adamson. Marilyn's big production number was 'Diamonds Are A Girl's Best Friend', sung – or breathed, perhaps – with an originality and a bouncy little-girl delight in the whole thing, which has the tune hanging in the air long

Marilyn Monroe and Jane Russell asserting their forceful personalities in Gentlemen Prefer Blondes.

after she has finished. Jane's own full-blooded solo was another Carmichael/Adamson number, 'Ain't There Anyone Here for Love?', and both women sang 'Bye Bye Baby' by Styne and Robin.

Marilyn did well in her musical numbers partly because she got on well and worked sympathetically with the film's musical director, Lionel Newman, and choreographer, Jack Cole. With its director, Howard Hawks, she was constantly at war, backed up by the unyielding critical opinion of Natasha Lytess. Hawks had the dubious distinction of being the first of numerous directors to find themselves at war with the Monroe drama coaches.

Fortunately for Marilyn's future career, there were among the big powers at Twentieth Century-Fox people sufficiently clear-sighted to see beyond the rather cool critical reception for her performance in *Gentlemen Prefer Blondes*

to the fact that the little blonde cutie was creating a strong style of her own. The question was whether it was big enough to survive the CinemaScope treatment.

This wide-screen process, perfected by a Frenchman, and bought up by Twentieth Century-Fox for use as a counter to the ever-growing menace of television, had been used by the studio to film a spectacular Biblical epic, *The Robe*, which would be a huge commercial success for them from the time it opened in New York in September 1953.

Now Fox were looking for a different kind of film to which they could apply the CinemaScope process. What worried everyone was whether subjects needing more intimate treatment, close-ups, ordinary indoor scenes and the like, would take successfully to wide-screen projection. There was a great deal of money to be lost if they failed.

Fine feathers make fine birds, and so do glittering, sequin-covered red dresses: Monroe and Russell in Gentlemen Prefer Blondes.

Marilyn Monroe taking a close interest in Tommy Noonan in Gentlemen Prefer Blondes.

Eventually, they chose to follow *The Robe* with a sophisticated comedy, *How to Marry a Millionaire*. They had to buy the film rights to three separate works to do it – one non-fiction work by a society writer for the title only, then two Broadway plays, 'The Greeks Had a Word for It' by Zoe Atkins and 'Loco' by Katherine Albert and Dale Eunsor for most of the plot. Nunnally Johnson, producer/writer of *We're Not Married*, did the screenplay

and Jean Negulesco, the Rumanian-born director of such fine films as *Johnny Belinda* and *Three Came Home*, was to direct.

The film was about the efforts of three good-looking models to catch herself a millionaire for a husband. The studio's choice for the stars of the movie were Monroe, Betty Grable and Lauren Bacall.

Naturally, the more sensation-seeking newspapers greeted the announcement of the casting of Grable and Monroe in the same picture as heralding a Battle of the Blondes. Jealous fighting on set was predicted between the thirty-seven-year-old Grable, once so important to Twentieth Century-Fox that they had insured her legs with Lloyds of London for a million dollars, and Monroe. It was surely only natural for Grable to feel jealous of the younger woman, knowing that the fan mail which had once flooded into the studio for her was now just a trickle and that she, and not Monroe, had originally been intended for the part of Lorelei Lee in *Gentlemen Prefer Blondes*. She probably knew, too, that Monroe was to get top billing in *Millionaire*.

All the signs of fame that had once been Grable's due were now being heaped on Marilyn. She and Jane Russell had put their feet and hand prints in concrete outside Grauman's Chinese Theater. (Did Gladys, now in a private sanatorium for which Marilyn was paying, hear and rejoice? Aunt Ana, who had died in 1948, would probably not have been all that impressed.) *Photoplay*, the nation's leading fan magazine, would vote her the most promising new star of 1953, an ironic award for a girl who had been making movies for seven years, though they would make amends in 1954 by voting her another Photoplay Gold Medal Award as the most popular actress of the year. The first Photoplay award, incidentally, was the occasion that sparked off Joan Crawford's bitter comments about Hollywood actresses who were not ladies. She thought that Marilyn's skin-tight, low-cut, gold lamé dress was a disgrace, a view with which, unfortunately, Joe DiMaggio agreed.

Celebrating with Mr. Bill Goetz his winning of a 1954 Achievement Award in recognition of his development of new talent.

Opposite: *Marilyn and Jane study the words and music of 'Two Little Girls From Little Rock'* which they sang together in Gentlemen Prefer Blondes.

Left: *Veteran moviemaker Howard Hawks directed* Gentlemen Prefer Blondes. *Here, he has an on-set discussion with Marilyn.*

Such rumblings did not mar the relationships between the stars of *How to Marry a Millionaire*. In the event, everyone was proved wrong, just as they had been wrong about Marilyn and Jane Russell, who had got on wonderfully well together, both on and off set. Jane and Marilyn had discussed love and marriage, life, literature and philosophy. If Betty Grable and Marilyn did not go to quite these lengths together, they still got on fine.

Marilyn is reported to have been concerned that the spectacles she was called on to wear in the film would be a big put-off. She need not have worried, for nothing, least of all a pair of horn-rimmed glasses, could dim the radiant, glowing sex appeal she projected in *How to Marry a Millionaire*. At last, all the hard work, all the grind, the intense expenditure of sheer will to succeed, jelled completely. She was wonderful.

How to Marry a Millionaire is all about that charming Hollywood cliché, the gold-digger with a heart, if not of gold, then at least in the right place. This time there are three of them, each of whom has decided that the only true way to achieve happiness in this world is to marry a millionaire.

Marilyn plays Pola Debevoise, a lovely, shapely and extremely short-sighted girl who joins forces with Loco Dempsey (Betty Grable) and Schatze Page (Lauren Bacall) to rent an expensive penthouse

An image that caught the imagination of the world: this skin-tight gold lamé dress with its plunging halter neckline became an essential part of the image and the myth of Marilyn Monroe.

apartment in New York, which they plan to use as a sort of spider's web in which to catch three millionaire flies.

Unfortunately, none of the girls turns out to be tough enough to play this game, and love keeps breaking in to disturb the smooth flow of their plans.

First of all, it is the elegant, stylish Schatze who goes temporarily off the rails, allowing herself to feel a considerable interest in a nice young man, Tom Brookman (Cameron Mitchell) who helps Loco carry her groceries in one day. But Schatze firmly hardens her heart; she must have no time for impecunious young men, even if they do possess one of the most charming smiles she has ever seen. Fortunately, Loco comes up with a genuine oil millionaire, the pleasant if somewhat elderly J.D. Hanley (William Powell), who takes a great interest in Schatze.

Then Loco misjudges both a wealthy and married businessman Waldo Brewster (Fred Clark) and her own ability to wander off down the paths of immorality. She takes a trip with Brewster, thinking

that they are off to a business convention in Maine, but the venue turns out to be a secluded forest lodge and the convention to consist of two people – her and him. Disillusioned, she decides to return to New York, but comes down with measles which means that she must stay where she is, though at least her honour is safe. While she is recovering, she meets an attractive forest ranger, Eben (Rory Calhoun) and, her resistance brought low by fever, falls in love with him.

Pola, meanwhile, has met a very smooth gentleman with a black patch over one eye, about whom she starts having some interesting fantasies. This is J. Stewart Merrill (Alex D'Arcy), and soon she is arranging to meet him in Atlantic City, there to be introduced to his mother, with a view to a long-term relationship. Since she will not wear her spectacles in public, Pola has not really noticed what she might be letting herself in for with the rather drippy-looking Mr. Merrill.

In the event, she never makes it to Atlantic City, for she shortsightedly mis-

Three very beautiful spiders sitting in the apartment/web in which they hope to ensnare a millionaire fly or two: Lauren Bacall, Betty Grable and Marilyn Monroe in How to Marry a Millionaire *(1953).*

reads the directions at the airport and boards the wrong aircraft. She finds herself sitting next to a pleasant, bespectacled man called Freddie Denmark (David Wayne), who turns out to be the landlord of her New York apartment block. He is on his way to sort out his business affairs with his tax accountant, who has managed to get him into trouble with the Revenue people. Since he wears glasses himself, Freddie does not mind about girls wearing them also, and soon Pola is feeling more comfortable with a man than she has ever done before.

Meanwhile, Schatze left alone in New York, decides she had better settle for Mr. Hanley and has got the wedding all arranged when Loco turns up with Eben. Both are brimming over with love for each other. Pola, when she arrives back in New York, has gone one better and is actually sporting a wedding ring, having already married Freddie. The others are not quite sure what her catch is like, though he seems pleasant enough, since Freddie sorted out his tax accountant to such effect that he is now wearing a neck brace and an assortment of bandages.

When it comes to the point Schatze finds that she really loves Tom, a fact which has become obvious to Mr. Hanley who, gentleman that he is, steps aside to make way for true love to triumph.

Once everything is sorted out, the three impecunious couples go off for a meal in a cheap diner (sauce bottles on the counter), where Tom causes a sensation by pulling out a very large wad of notes indeed with

Happy line-up at the première of How to Marry a Millionaire: *with Lauren Bacall is her husband Humphrey Bogart, and Marilyn Monroe is squired by the film's producer Nunnally Johnson.*

which to pay the bill. Schatze will have a monied marriage after all. And so they all live happily ever after.

'What a smash for Twentieth Century-Fox', cheered *Variety* in its review of the CinemaScope *How to Marry a Millionaire*. 'The studio has a rollicking smartly sophisticated comedy that will delight audiences . . . . It is a superbly acted and directed laugh riot. The performers are consistently brilliant, Miss Monroe getting howls with her near-sighted gropings.'

On paper, Marilyn did not have any bigger a part in *How to Marry a Millionaire* than the other two female stars, but on screen, she generally looked the biggest, most important character, though Lauren Bacall's stylish playing grabbed a few scenes from her. When Marilyn was on screen, comically awkward and bumbling but also – dazzling contrast – gorgeously voluptuous as well, you did not look at anyone else, and when she was off you kept waiting for her to reappear.

Was she acting, or was she just being herself? In this film, she proved triumphantly that it did not matter. Whatever it was in the chemical make-up of Miss Marilyn Monroe that turned to dynamite on screen when caught on film, it was certainly the most effective force around in Hollywood in 1953.

Within three months of its release, *Gentlemen Prefer Blondes* had taken more than $2 million dollars at the American box office alone, and it was clear from the outset that *How to Marry a Millionaire* would do even better.

There would be several months' gap between Marilyn's completion of her work on *How to Marry a Millionaire* and the film's release in November 1953, so Twentieth Century-Fox, intent on keeping her before the public gaze and the money rolling in, set her to work on a drama/adventure story set in the wilds of the Canadian Rockies. This was *River of No Return*, a sort of northern Western, given the full Fox treatment with CinemaScope and Technicolor.

It is supposed to be the worst film the mature film star Monroe made, and just about the worst that Otto Preminger ever directed, a view probably spread more by the two principals, who ended up hating the film and each other, than by cinema-

During filming of River of No Return *(1954) Marilyn badly twisted a ligament in her foot. Here, an anxious Otto Preminger, the film's director, ensures that his valuable star can cope safely with her crutches.*

goers and critics. It is a reasonably entertaining movie – not good, but not too bad either. Monroe was not right for the part, that is undeniable: she was never much good playing tough, dangerous women, and she neither looked nor acted convincingly. Her make-up was too careful, too sophisticated, for either the plot or the scenic background, and she looked faintly odd dressed in jeans and a shirt.

Since a good part of the plot had her and co-star Robert Mitchum struggling down river on a raft, it was also a physically dangerous and exhausting film. During filming of one scene, Monroe slipped off the raft and, according to several newspapers, 'nearly drowned' when the fishing waders she was wearing

Opposite: *A glamorously seductive Marilyn in one of the slinky gowns she wore in* How to Marry a Millionaire.

Below: *Fantasy looms large for Marilyn and Alex D'Arcy in this scene from* How to Marry a Millionaire.

to protect her costume filled with water and dragged her down in the river. This sounds to be a bit of journalistic licence, but there is no doubt that she was shaken and hurt, for she badly pulled a ligament in one foot. She telephoned Joe DiMaggio down in California and he, pausing only long enough to collect a doctor, rushed up to Canada to look after her. Marilyn was deeply touched by this, and before *River of No Return* was completed, she had agreed to marry him. They set a date for some time in January 1954.

Completion of the film was not easy, for Marilyn came to dislike and distrust Otto Preminger very much. He felt much the same way about her and even worse about poor Natasha Lytess, who had come to Canada in Marilyn's train as she had been on every film set since *Clash by Night*.

The story of *River of No Return* has Marilyn playing Kay, a good-time girl, a saloon-bar singer and the girlfriend of a gambler called Harry Weston (Rory Calhoun). Through a young boy she talks to called Mark (Tommy Rettig), Kay meets farmer Matt Calder (Robert Mitchum), Mark's father and a man with a prison record: he once shot a man in the back and, although there were extenuating circumstances, he has not told Mark.

Matt meets up with Kay again when he rescues her and Harry Weston from potential danger in the river near his farm. They are hurrying to town to register a gold claim and Harry, intent on his gold, steals Matt's only horse to get him to town fast. The other three are now stranded, and Indians are planning an attack. The only way out of their present danger is down the river, a hazardous undertaking in itself. They meet and overcome many dangers, though Mark seems to reject his father when Kay, in a rage brought about by fear and exhaustion, reveals to Mark the 'truth' about his father. Matt cannot

convince his son that his act was not a totally evil one.

Once safely in town, they catch up with Harry and, inevitably there is a fight in which Kay is involved. Having come to love Matt for his essential decency, she tries to persuade Harry not to fight him. In the end, to save her, young Mark is forced to shoot Harry Weston in the back. There are some more misunderstandings to clear up before Kay, redeemed by the love of a good man, goes off with him and Mark to start a new life.

Not much of a story, really, and Milton Luban was about right when he wrote in the *Hollywood Reporter* that *River of No Return* was entertaining enough to be a box office natural, though 'its potential is marred by its choice of the top female role. If 'River' proves anything at all it is that Marilyn Monroe should stick to musicals and the type of entertainments that made her such a box-office lure . . . most of her genuine values are lost here.'

On the other hand, Mr. Luban added, the casting of Robert Mitchum had been pure inspiration, with him giving the finest performance of his career to date. Mr. Luban had made a big point: it is a real pleasure to see Marilyn at last being given a truly attractive, sexy man as her on-screen partner, and being allowed to keep him in the last reel. (*Four* films with that nice nonentity, David Wayne, for goodness sake!)

Marilyn sang four songs in the film, the title song which she sang winningly to Tommy Rettig, 'I'm Gonna File My Claim', 'One Silver Dollar' and 'Down in the Meadow', all by Ken Darby and Lionel Newman. She gave a good account of all of them, in her inimitable, little-girl breath-ful voice, and a record of one of them, 'I'm Gonna File My Claim', sold 75,000 copies in three weeks when it was released in the U.S.A. in 1954. It was not her first recording success, for 'Diamonds Are A Girl's Best Friend' from *Gentlemen Prefer Blondes* reached the top of the United States Hit Parade in mid-1953.

River of No Return had been a bad experience for Marilyn, and she returned to Los Angeles in a truculent mood. Twentieth Century-Fox, unwilling to let up on such a dazzlingly successful financial winner for them, were proposing more films for immediate production. Unfortunately, they chose to tell the world before they told Marilyn that she was about to start work on a confection called *The Girl in Pink Tights*, for which they had signed up Frank Sinatra at a salary grossly in excess of hers, to play opposite her. And, no, Miss Monroe

could not see the script: all she had to do was show up for work.

Marilyn put her pretty little foot down. She did not like her low salary, she disliked the film's script, once she saw it, very much indeed, and she would not do it. Fox suspended her from the payroll.

Marilyn, her self-confidence never very securely balanced, nearly backed down. But Joe swept her doubts aside. He was not very impressed by her movie career anyway – he had not even accompanied her to the spectacular première of *How to Marry a Millionaire* and she, the great star, had gone alone – and he apparently quite seriously thought that she would largely give it up in favour of a home and a large family once they were married. He told Marilyn to forget about the studio and to start thinking about marrying him instead.

So, 1953 ended for Marilyn with her a happily engaged girl and the biggest box-office success in Hollywood – on suspension. She could take comfort from the fact that a nation-wide poll of film men, critics and cinema owners showed that in not much more than a year she had risen from very little to being fifth in the list of 'America's favourite stars', after Gary Cooper, who was top, Bing Crosby, Ava Gardner and Susan Hayward; following Marilyn into sixth place was John Wayne. She had arrived.

Left: *No sign of how unhappy she was working on* River of No Return *shows on Marilyn's face as she swings gaily from the step of a train for a publicity shot.*

Opposite: *Marilyn Monroe provided the glamour when she was guest star on Jack Benny's first show of his 1953 season on CBS television. The show's producer Ralph Levy keeps an eye on the camera angles.*

A Sex Symbol
Is Just a Thing

Marilyn Monroe and Joe DiMaggio were married in San Francisco on 14 January 1954. Because Joe did not like low-cut clothes on his woman, she wore a high-necked frock, dressed up with an ermine collar and flowers. He wore a conservative dark suit with a white carnation in the buttonhole. There were a few friends, a great many more photographers and reporters, and the happy couple obliged with a kiss for their fans to see reproduced in newspapers all over the world.

Although they were the most famous married couple in America, they managed to get a honeymoon quite alone, with few people even recognizing them as they drove into the high, snow-covered mountains near Palm Springs. The bride was no doubt made even happier when she learned that Twentieth Century-Fox had lifted their suspension order on her. The studio probably considered how bad it would have looked if they had continued to play the heavy-handed boss in the face of such a fine romance.

Early in February, Mr. and Mrs. DiMaggio flew to Japan, where Joe had business to conduct. It was Mrs. DiMaggio, needless to say, who attracted all the attention. They were mobbed in Hawaii, where they changed planes; they were mobbed again when they reached Japan, and had to escape from the aircraft through the luggage hatch. People reached out to touch her, even to grab at her, at her hair, her clothing. He was pretty much ignored. It was frightening for her, and doubly demoralizing for him: in the first place, he was unable to protect her as a strong husband should, and secondly, he, America's greatest baseball player and a sportsman of world stature, was not considered to have any more importance in events than their luggage. When Mar-

ilyn went on to Korea, at the invitation of an army general who had been on their flight to Japan, she went alone.

U.S. troops had first landed in South Korea in 1950, and were now, in 1954, overseeing the armistice line which had been agreed to in 1953. A morale-boosting visit from the girl a whole battalion of U.S. soldiers in Korea had once volunteered to marry would surely do nothing but good, even though the girl was now married – and not to a soldier. And so it proved. Even touring around dressed in padded Army jackets against the Korean cold, she looked blonde, beautiful and highly desirable. When she stood up on a makeshift stage in front of them, heroically wearing low-cut dresses in the cold wind, they loved her. At last, the girl who had been in front of them in pin-up form for years was there in the flesh, and they were not disappointed. Her four-day visit was an enormous success.

It also reminded her, if she needed reminding, that she was Marilyn Monroe first and Mrs. Joseph DiMaggio second. Joe did not see it that way, of course, nor was he overly impressed by her tales of the cheers and adulation of thousands of American boys in Korea. He had heard plenty of cheering for himself in his time.

Back in America, things did not improve, and there were soon rumours circulating that all was not well in the DiMaggio households – both of them, for they had to set up two homes, one in San Francisco where they were part of the lively, wide-ranging DiMaggio family life, and one in Los Angeles to use when Marilyn was filming, a business that left Joe too much alone with nothing to do.

The film Marilyn Monroe began making in mid-1954, after several months absence from the world of the film

For years Marilyn Monroe had been a pin-up for US troops in Korea; now, in February 1954, the living, breathing, sexily wonderful real thing is before them. Her visit is a triumph.

studios, was *There's No Business Like Show Business*, a musical tribute to the composing genius of Irving Berlin. Marilyn was cast opposite the amiable song-and-dance comedian Donald O'Connor – in size, at least, no improvement at all on Frank Sinatra, with whom she should have made a film that year. He was not exactly an important leading man either: he was sandwiching his part in *Show Business* between two more tales in his popular, though feeble, Francis-the-talking-mule series. Also in the cast were dancer Dan Dailey, Mitzi Gaynor, singer Johnnie Ray and that high-octane performer, Ethel Merman, who could belt out a song like no other. Marilyn, not an expert singer or dancer, was out of her depth in a cast where all the other leading players were, and it showed. Apparently, she had not cared for the project from the outset and only took it as part of an agreement which allowed her *The Seven Year Itch* as a follow-up.

There's No Business Like Show Business is a back-stage story, with plenty of on-stage scenes. It is about a show business song-and-dance family, the Donahues, led by Molly (Ethel Merman) and Terry (Dan Dailey) who with their three children Tim (Donald O'Connor), Katy (Mitzi

Gaynor) and Steve (Johnnie Ray) are billed as The Five Donahues.

Unfortunately the children, having grown up, begin to go their own ways, and the troupe starts to fall apart. Tim has set eyes on the love of his life, a beautiful young blonde, Vicky Hoffman (Monroe), a girl with thespian aspirations and a pear-shaped accent to match, working as a hat-check girl in a night club while trying to break into show business. When Tim next meets Vicky she has changed her name to Parker, dropped the phony accent, and got herself a cabaret job, on the same bill as the Donahues in a Miami hotel.

Tim's efforts to further Vicky's career cause dissension in the family especially when she performs a song called 'Heat Wave', which the Donahues should have done. Then Tim starts to suspect, mistakenly as it turns out, that Vicky is showing too much interest in the show's producer Lew Harris (Richard Eastham), and goes off the rails, getting so drunk he is involved in a car accident which lands him, not too badly hurt, in hospital. It is opening night and he should, of course, be on stage.

All this trouble in the family is too much for father, Terry, and he stops taking part in the act altogether. Tim, in the meantime, has also disappeared. The show must go on, and Molly, trouper that she is, keeps what is left of the act together, working with daughter Katy, and retaining very bitter feelings towards Vicky whom she regards as the cause of all their misfortunes.

In the end, as in all good, sentimental back-stage stories, everything turns out well, hatchets are buried and all the family are reunited on stage with Vicky, who is now going to marry Tim, for a big production number, 'There's No Business Like Show Business' which spreads itself nicely across the CinemaScope screen.

The best thing about this rather trite and hackneyed tale was that it allowed room for many of Irving Berlin's best songs, which meant that *There's No Business Like Show Business* was at least an entertaining enough film, with sufficient bounce and pep, and a topping of nostalgia to keep audiences happy.

Well, not entirely happy, in fact, for one of Marilyn's three big production numbers, 'Heat Wave', had her wearing a ridiculous costume, vaguely suggestive of Carmen Miranda. Its frilled skirt, split high enough to show her black briefs when she danced, was thought by many to be objectionably suggestive and caused a considerable amount of criticism. She herself had found the number difficult and had many arguments with the film's choreographer, Robert Alton. Her other two songs in the film were 'Lazy' and 'After you get What you Want, you Don't Want It'.

So unsure was she of her own ability to do the part that she put in hours of extra coaching on top of the long filming schedule. The result back in the DiMaggio Hollywood home was a tired, short-tempered bride and a husband who was beginning to feel that he did not have a bride at all – or, at least, not one who showed any signs of turning into a wife and mother.

Reviews for the film as a piece of cinema entertainment were favourable on the whole. *There's No Business Like Show Business* was a typical Twentieth Century-Fox production: loud, highly-coloured, fairly brash and lacking the smooth sophistication that was the hallmark of the best M.G.M. musicals, for instance. Thus,

Monroe in effervescent mood.

for those critics who did not like it, words like vulgar, over-produced, tasteless, and cheap turned up again and again in reviews. 'A vulgar picture', wrote C.A. Lejeune in *The Observer* in London, 'suggesting to me at least an insult to intelligence, religion, music, Ethel Merman, good taste and the human soul'.

Those who did like it managed to give the impression that they did so despite its vulgarity, cheapness etc, like Virginia Graham in the British weekly, *The Spectator* who commented that Twentieth Century-Fox, 'has sprung full-armed to the challenge of television with a musical which is splitting at the seams with talent. . . . . The numbers are all gigantic, spectacular, hideously coloured and a bit on the messy side, but it is impossible not to be stimulated by such a display of energy, not to be dazzled by the assembly of talents giving their shining all. A battering but cheerful experience'.

Marilyn came in for a considerable amount of criticism, much of it directed at the cheap sexiness of her performance. Monroe's recent remark that she would like to play in *The Brothers Karamazov* didn't help matters and was used as a stick to hit at what seemed vulgar pretension on her part. Bosley Crowther in the *New York Times* found her 'wriggling and squirming to "Heat Wave" and "Lazy" . . . embarrassing to behold', while Roy Nash in the London *Star*, thought that her rendition of 'Lazy', 'lolling on a sofa as if she has just fallen in love with it, ridiculous'. Other reviewers came to the more thoughtful conclusion that her vulgarity was as much the studio's and director Walter Lang's fault as hers. 'If they would stop working so hard to make this girl sexy, Twentieth Century-Fox might discover Miss Monroe is a good actress with authentic comic gifts', said the British *Saturday Review* while Kate Cameron in the *New York Daily News* noted, as did other critics, a certain comic sending-up of her role in Monroe's performance; 'she does a comic burlesque of the sexy singer of naughty songs'. In fact, her singing of three Irving Berlin numbers in her soft voice, variously described as being like marshmallow, raspberry mousse and other confections, is uniquely attractive: perhaps better enjoyed when listened to on a record rather than in the cinema. Maybe Mr. Bosley Crowther should have shut his eyes and just lis-

Right: *Improving on perfection. Final adjustments are made to Marilyn's make-up and costume before she steps in front of the camera on the set of* There's No Business Like Show Business *(1954).*

Opposite: *The spotlight is on Miss Vicky Parker, alias Marilyn Monroe, as the show goes on in* There's No Business Like Show Business.

Donald O'Connor,
Marilyn Monroe and
Mitzi Gaynor with their
interpretations of 'Lazy'
in There's No Business
Like Show Business.

tened: after all, Mr. Irving Berlin thought that Monroe's treatment of his songs was better than all right – a revelation to him, in fact.

Finally, one review from a popular British daily probably sums up better than most the average film-goer's not too sophisticated requirements of the movies he goes to: 'Much of Berlin's music is old . . . and what is musically new seems to me inferior except when Miss Monroe is singing it', wrote the *News Chronicle*'s film critic. 'I don't care whether she is wearing feathers that erupt from her head like the Yellowstone Geyser, or the black three-quarter-length slacks unfunction-ally adorned by a pale blue sash, in which she addresses a gold telephone from a scarlet *chaise longue*. I only know that whereas the rest of the talented cast succumb to their material, she alone rises above it; and that there's no business like Monroe business.'

Fortunately, by the time *There's No Business Like Show Business* was released in the States at the end of 1954, Marilyn had already completed work on her next film, *The Seven Year Itch*, so that the poor *Show Business* reviews could not affect her confidence in her work in *The Seven Year Itch*.

Since filming of *There's No Business Like Show Business* had gone way over schedule – partly because Marilyn had collapsed from exhaustion on the set several times and had had to be given time off – there was no time for a pause to allow the DiMaggios to get themselves back on the same track again before Marilyn began filming *The Seven Year Itch*.

This film, whose theme Marilyn, her big grey-blue eyes innocently wide, said she had never understood when she was asked about it a couple of years later, was about the doubts, worries and fantasies that hit a man in his marriage when the early romance has worn off to be replaced by familiarity and boredom with his life's partner. In a wider context, the film is also concerned with sexual infidelity and emotional insecurity – feelings manifested, in the husband's mind, by jealous doubts about the relationship between his wife and their best friend.

The task of putting *The Seven Year Itch*, originally a successful Broadway play by George Axelrod, on to film was given to Billy Wilder, a brilliant and sensitive screenwriter and director, one of whose most recent big successes had been *Sunset Boulevard*, for which he had co-authored the screenplay with Charles Brackett. The part of the husband, Richard Sherman, was played by the same actor who had made a success of the role on the Broadway stage, Tom Ewell. He had also made a successful screen debut playing opposite Judy Holliday in *Adam's Rib* and seemed the ideal choice to turn in a good performance in *The Seven Year Itch*.

Marilyn Monroe was a natural for the part of the beautiful, if slightly vacuous, blonde actress from the apartment upstairs. Given no name, she is referred to on the cast list simply as The Girl, as if she were intended to be, not a person, but a symbol of the sort of thing men are supposed to itch for.

The story of *The Seven Year Itch* is set in New York, mostly in a typical apartment block where Richard Sherman, a publisher, is left alone for the summer while his wife Helen (Evelyn Keyes) and their small son Ricky (Butch Bernard) go off to Maine on vacation. Richard, a man with a strong Walter Mitty streak, meets the girl from the apartment upstairs when she rings his bell to get into the building, having forgotten her key. Her splendid figure and lovely face spark off some interesting fantasies in Richard's mind, which are intensified when she accidentally knocks a pot plant on to his terrace, nearly braining him as he sits reading a book, and he invites her down to his apartment to have a drink. She is an out-of-town innocent and he shows his sophistication by playing a record of Rachmaninov: it should be a seductive piece, but The Girl disarms him completely by remarking, 'That's what they call classical music, isn't it? I could tell because there's

no vocal'. Later she suggests that his carefully mixed martini could do with some sugar.

So keyed up is he that he tries to make a pass at her, even though she has announced that she feels perfectly safe with married men. Since they are both sitting on the piano stool, picking out chopsticks on the keyboard when Richard makes his pass, they both fall off the stool and end up on the floor.

Despite the embarrassment of this incident, Richard continues to fantasize about The Girl after she had gone back upstairs. He imagines her lying in a bubble bath with her toe caught in the tap. She has to call in a plumber (Victor Moore), to whom she naturally passes on the story. Worse, when she does a toothpaste ad on television she then tells her television audience all about Richard's libertine behaviour . . . .

Marilyn in costume for her controversial 'Heat Wave' number in There's No Business Like Show Business.

Pulling himself together, Richard decides to act like any normal male and ask The Girl out for the evening. They have dinner and go to the cinema (*Creature from the Black Lagoon*, in fact). As they are on their way back to the apartment block The Girl stops in Lexington Avenue to stand on a subway grating, allowing the deliciously cool breeze coming from it every time a train rumbles past to blow around her, wafting the pleated skirt of her dress up into the air.

The Girl is still in search of cooling breezes when they get home, and asks if she can spend the night in his apartment, where the conditioning is working well. He is reluctant and alarmed, but finally gives her the bedroom while he apparently sleeps in the living room. Naturally, his imagination takes off into the stratosphere again, his fantasies including a scene in which his wife, Helen, finds out about his apparent infidelities, and murders him.

Morning brings real trouble for Richard when a family friend, Tom MacKenzie (Sonny Tufts), just drops by to pick up something to take back to Helen at the resort where they are both staying. The Girl is in the kitchen. Richard imagines the worst when he sees Tom carrying out a seemingly quite intimate little task for Helen, and impulsively K.O.s poor Tom. Richard realizes that he has allowed everything to get out of proportion. Summer in New York obviously does not agree with him, so he decides that he had better join his wife on holiday. He offers his air-conditioned apartment to The Girl, who accepts, delightedly giving him a kiss of thanks that also manages to indicate that she has come to like him, ineffective goof as he may seem, very much indeed, not as a male sex object but as a human being. When he leaves, still in turmoil, The Girl has to throw his shoes after him.

The Seven Year Itch was a deliciously funny, witty and thoroughly entertaining film, and was a great box-office success both for Marilyn Monroe and for Twentieth Century-Fox. Billy Wilder turned out to have exactly the right technique for dealing with an actress of Monroe's sensi-

123

tivity and whose lack of confidence needed constant care and attention. Wilder was also clever enough to use Natasha Lytess to his advantage, rather than setting up his will against hers and Marilyn's. The result was a relatively easy run during the shooting of the film.

For the average daily newspaper critic, forced to produce an instant, off-the-cuff, ready-for-the-first-edition review, *The Seven Year Itch* was a pleasure to sit through, as it was, of course, for most of the fans. 'The funniest and most intelligent farce of the year', said London's *Standard*. For *The Spectator*, Tom Ewell gives 'a wonderful comedy performance. So, too, somewhat surprisingly, is Marilyn Monroe's . . . she radiates a ludicrous innocence which is completely bewitching'. For Philip Strassberg in the *New York Daily Mirror*, the film was well worth waiting for. 'Tom Ewell . . . and La Monroe deserve most of

the credit for carrying off the comedy coup.' As for Monroe, 'a fine comedienne', her 'pouting delivery, puckered lips . . . make her one of Hollywood's top attractions which she again proves here'.

The Times in London saw Miss Monroe going serenely on with her transformation from pin-up girl into actress. 'There is a charming air of ingenuous innocence about this disturber of poor Richard's good resolutions and peace of mind . . . She is a being marvellously devoid of the normal processes of thought, and Miss Monroe plays her with a wide-eyed amusement that stops on the right side of self-parody. If Miss Monroe goes on like this, the day when she appears as Lady Macbeth cannot be long delayed.'

Goodness! – and she had not yet even attended Mr. Lee Strasberg's acting classes in New York. Milton Shulman, in the *Sunday Express*, was much more down to earth than the high-minded *Times*, and

concentrated on Monroe, purveyor of sex appeal:

'The test of a great film actress is whether or not she can bring something unique and individual to the imposing matter of sex.

'Mary Pickford brought it innocence. Theda Bara made it exotic. Marlene Dietrich made it unapproachable. Ginger Rogers gave it gaiety. Joan Crawford made it miserable, Garbo lifted it to the spiritual. Ava Gardner brought it down to earth.

'By this standard Miss Marilyn Monroe has certainly wiggled herself a niche in Hollywood's hall of fame. For she has made sex very funny . . . . Surveying her, one is forced to grin at one's own imagination. She converts a wolf whistle into a wry chuckle.'

For the film critic and movie writer with time to stop and think about all the implications of the film version of *The*

Seven Year Itch, it is far from being Billy Wilder's most successful film. He himself has said that he would like the property back to do all over again. Censorship at the time meant he could not do the right and obvious thing by the story and let Richard Sherman and The Girl from upstairs have an affair. The lack of a real affair left the theme unresolved, the film without a centre, and the character of Richard too indecisive. The general negativeness of the Richard Sherman character is only heightened by the casting of Monroe as The Girl. Although it is hard to agree with the opinion of *The New Yorker* that 'when Miss Monroe turns up as a young lady too substantial for dreams, the picture is reduced to the level of a burlesque show', it has to be admitted that she dominates the film too much for the story's good.

None of this mattered to Twentieth Century-Fox when they saw the rushes of *The Seven Year Itch*. They knew they had

The Girl upstairs takes a bubble bath in The Seven Year Itch.

Director Billy Wilder and Marilyn discuss their next moves between takes of The Seven Year Itch.

a winner, and so did Marilyn. She knew, too, that she had given a fine, subtle performance, indicating the warm, sensitive woman behind the dizzy, simple blonde exterior.

The difference between the Marilyn of *Show Business* and the Marilyn of *The Seven Year Itch* was remarkable. In the former, she looked jaded, and casting her opposite the perennially youthful Donald O'Connor had not helped: she looked like mutton dressed as lamb. The sparkle

seemed to have gone. Turn to *The Seven Year Itch,* and the sparkle, the sheer joy in living, has returned. She looks ebullient, carefree, bubbling with health and vitality.

What makes the performance even more remarkable is the realization that the woman behind the actress was suffering the traumatic experience of having her marriage break up. Many commentators have pin-pointed that famous scene of The Girl standing on the subway grating as the point of no return in the Monroe-DiMaggio marriage.

Joe had come, reluctantly, to New York to be with Marilyn and had watched the filming of the scene. It was done in the early hours, when New York should have been asleep and the streets deserted. Instead, news of the filming had leaked out and a sizeable crowd, including many newsmen and photographers, gathered to watch. Smart, sophisticated New York, or at least its media, had been thrown into an extraordinarily unsophisticated tizzy by the presence of Monroe in the city (just as the population and media of smart, sophisticated, old-world-cultured London would be two years later when she turned up to film *The Prince and the Showgirl*).

The presence of so many people – at least 4,000 according to some reports – at the filming was another sign of the near-hysteria that Monroe had aroused in New York, especially among its menfolk, a large number of whom were now smacking their lips, whistling and making many pretty basic remarks at the sight of Mrs. Joe DiMaggio showing her legs and her underwear for the benefit of anyone who liked to look – or so it seemed to Mr. Joe DiMaggio. He was, from all accounts, sickened and disgusted by the whole episode. He still loved Marilyn, the girl he had married and, indeed, he would continue to care about her until she died and for many years afterwards, but he hated the fact that his wife was also a sex symbol, a piece of public property. He wanted her to give it up, to stay at home, have children, maybe even learn to make pasta like every right-thinking, good-living Italian-American girl. It was obviously impossible, and the tensions created by their diverging needs made divorce inevitable.

The announcement of the break-up came when Marilyn still had several weeks of work to complete on *The Seven Year Itch* in Hollywood. The news was like an explosion, ripping its way through the gossip columns of America. The newsmen gathered at the DiMaggio house, waiting for something to report. Eventually, they were rewarded by the sight of first Joe leaving, luggage in hand, for his home in San Francisco, then of Marilyn, weeping, handkerchief in hand, being led out by her lawyer. Only a week after the announcement, she was back at work, surprising Wilder by the professionalism of her performance. *The Seven Year Itch* was completed without mishap.

In November 1954 Marilyn Monroe was granted an interlocutory divorce from Joe DiMaggio on the grounds of mental cruelty. The marriage had lasted less than ten months and Joe did not contest the divorce. It would seem from what came out at a quite different legal case two years later, though, that Joe DiMaggio at one time considered either contesting the divorce or cross-petitioning.

In February 1957 a hearing took place in Los Angeles before a California senate

Photographer Milton Greene made this study of his friend and later business partner in New York in 1954.

committee investigating charges that divorce detectives had been selling stories from their investigations to scandal magazines. In court was a private detective, Phil Irwin, and film star and singer Frank Sinatra. Irwin said that Sinatra had taken part in a raid on an apartment carried out by private detectives hired by Mr. Joe DiMaggio to obtain divorce evidence against Marilyn Monroe. Sinatra denied this. He said that although he had driven with DiMaggio to the house where Marilyn was supposed to have been staying, he had remained outside in the car and had taken no part in the raid. His testimony was backed up by DiMaggio, who confirmed that Sinatra had not gone into the house. No evidence of misbehaviour on

Marilyn's part was ever turned up. Indeed, the raid had gone farcically wrong, the detectives bursting into the wrong apartment and considerably alarming another lady, woken from sleep.

It was a rather ridiculous episode, leaving Joe for once in an ungentlemanly light, though Marilyn seems never to have held it against him or Sinatra, for she continued seeing and going about with both in the early 1960s after her divorce from Arthur Miller.

When Marilyn divorced Joe DiMaggio she had plans in mind that meant more than just staying on in Hollywood working out her contract with Twentieth Century-Fox. She, too, disliked and distrusted the sex symbol image: 'a sex

symbol becomes a thing; I hate being a thing', was one of her more famous remarks.

While working on *There's No Business Like Show Business* she had met two people in whom she saw a possible means of escape from the sex symbol image into a new career as an actress and a woman.

One was a photographer, Milton Greene, an attractive man for whom she felt an instant rapport. His suggestion that she should, with his help, establish her own film production company, Marilyn Monroe Productions Inc., which would have her acting talents as its greatest asset, found favour with her. She liked, too, his and his lawyer's belief that she could get out of her contract with Twentieth Century-Fox on several grounds and make a new deal with them.

Monroe was to mull over his ideas for some months. She also seriously considered the idea of going to New York to study at the Actors' Studio under the famous Lee Strasberg. His teaching of the

Stanislavsky Method of acting was having a profound effect on American theatre and cinema. Sidney Skolsky had introduced Marilyn to Lee Strasberg's wife, Paula, on the set of *Show Business* and Marilyn had been considerably impressed. Paula Strasberg was to have an enormous influence on Marilyn's later film career.

Marilyn apparently told no one in Hollywood of her plans and hopes for the future, secretly flying to New York at the end of 1954, perhaps fleeing from the bad reviews she got for *Show Business*, released in December. It would be six months before *The Seven Year Itch* would be released to redeem her reputation.

Meanwhile, she set about making a new and a different life for herself in New York. It seemed as though she was turning her back on Hollywood, an extraordinary and unprecedented thing for a film star and actress in her position to do. Twentieth Century-Fox, sure of their contract, sure of their hold over her, were disbelieving. It would be nearly a year before they

Right: *Milton Greene at work again. This study of Marilyn was taken in New York in 1956.*

Opposite: *Back on the West Coast in 1955, Milton Greene posed Marilyn in a natural setting for this portrait.*

would admit defeat and re-write her contract, an action which the success of *The Seven Year Itch* had a lot to do with, emphasizing as it did the enormous earning power of the Monroe name at the head of a cast list.

Monroe had been in New York only a few weeks when her new company, with her as president and holder of 51 per cent of the shares and Greene as vice-president with 49 per cent, was announced at a well-attended press conference. Soon, she had also met Lee Strasberg who agreed to give her private lessons before she entered regular classes at the Actors' Studio. The classes were radically to alter her approach to all her later screen roles as she put into practice the principles of the Method learned from Strasberg. She was not the first screen actor to do so, either – among Hollywood's more famous members of the Actors' Studio were Marlon Brando, Montgomery Clift, Rod Steiger, Shelley Winters and Paul Newman – it was just that she was the first 'dumb blonde' sex symbol to take the Method seriously.

The third important life-changing thing to happen to Marilyn Monroe was the development of her friendship with the left-thinking playwright Arthur Mil-

ler. They had already met in Los Angeles in 1951 but nothing much came of their meetings then, though neither forgot the other. Marilyn seems to have classed him in the same category as such men as Abraham Lincoln, a figure she felt such an admiration for that she usually had a print of him somewhere in her apartments or houses, generally over the bed.

Now she and Miller began seeing a lot of each other. She had not completely forgotten Joe DiMaggio, who escorted her to the New York première of *The Seven Year Itch* in mid-1955, but she had clearly stopped thinking that something might be saved of their marriage before the divorce became final. Now the man in her life was Arthur Miller. Since he was still married to his first wife, by whom he had two children, now teenagers, he and Monroe were very discreet about their relationship throughout Marilyn's East Coast summer and the remainder of 1955.

Marilyn as the shopworn singer Cherie in Bus Stop *(1956), her first film back in Hollywood after she went East to study at the Actors' Studio in New York.*

Monroe's New Year present for 1956 from Twentieth Century-Fox was a new contract, under which she agreed to make four films for them over a seven-year period. She would be paid the great sum of $100,000 per film, plus expenses, and would have script and director approval. She was also permitted under the terms of her contract to make at least one film a year independent of the studio and to take part in a certain number of television shows. After holding out for a year, Twentieth Century-Fox had caved in to the demands of the little blonde cutie in whom Darryl F. Zanuck had once seen no potential at all.

This year would see Marilyn Monroe reaching at least two summits of her great range of ambitions. As an actress, she played in two films. In the first, *Bus Stop*, she tackled successfully a role compounded of comedy and tragedy which proved her to be a genuinely talented actress. In the other, *The Prince and the Showgirl*, she acted opposite one of the world's greatest actors, a real Prince of the theatre, Laurence Olivier. The other summit was as a woman, when she 'proved' to the world her right to be taken seriously by marrying an admired member of the American intellectual establishment, Arthur Miller.

The film rights of Terence Rattigan's play, 'The Sleeping Prince', had been bought for Marilyn Monroe Productions Inc. by Milton Greene, Marilyn accepting without question his belief that the leading female part in it, played on the London stage by Olivier's wife, Vivien Leigh, would be perfect for her. The announcement that Monroe would make *The Sleeping Prince* (the film's title was not changed until just before it was due for distribution) in England after making *Bus Stop* in America, was made at a New York press conference, attended by Monroe, Olivier and Milton Greene. The assembled horde of journalists discovered that a year in New York learning to be a Method actress had turned the sexy blonde film star into something of a Grande Dame as well as a businesswoman who was president of her own company.

Within a month the businesswoman was back in Los Angeles for the first time in sixteen months, the longest absence from her place of birth she had ever

Monroe and Baddy Adler, producer of Bus Stop, *in sunny mood during the making of the film.*

experienced. She had left under a cloud of criticism for the cheap vulgarity of her role in *There's No Business Like Show Business*. She came back as a veritable Queen of Hollywood. Vast crowds of fans turned out at the airport to greet her, jostling the hordes of reporters and photographers there to record the scene. She would soon be thirty years old, and must have felt she had reached a turning point in her life.

As far as her next film went, she had. Her role in *Bus Stop* was very far removed from the self-confident, sexy girls she had played in her recent films. George Axelrod wrote the screenplay from the play of the same name by Pulitzer Prize-winning playwright William Inge, whose other plays adapted for the cinema included *Come Back Little Sheba* and *Picnic*. Joshua Logan, a playwright and highly regarded Broadway director who had only very recently taken to film directing (*Picnic* was his first solo directing film), was to direct the film, with Twentieth Century-Fox's Buddy Adler producing.

Logan could not have been a better choice. A finely sensitive director, he had himself studied under Stanislavsky at the Moscow Arts Theatre in the early 1930s, and therefore understood and appreciated what Monroe was trying to achieve in *Bus Stop* and why she went about things the way she did. Another Method-trained person on the *Bus Stop* set was Paula Strasberg who had now replaced Natasha Lytess as Marilyn's coach. Lytess was dropped without warning, without explanation, without thanks, both from Marilyn's life and from the Fox payroll.

Monroe and Logan had many long sessions discussing the film and its script before shooting began in Phoenix, Arizona in March 1956. Among their longest discussions was the question of who should play the leading male role in the film. Many of Hollywood's and Broadway's best actors were considered and rejected before the choice finally fell on the virtually unknown Don Murray, a stage actor who got his first, and his best, screen role playing opposite Marilyn.

Bus Stop is the story of an untalented, second-rate and decidedly shop-soiled

Marilyn sings 'That Old Black Magic' to an indifferent audience in Bus Stop.

singer reduced to singing in cafes where no one notices her. She is trying to make it to Los Angeles and fame and fortune, though it is pretty clear that she never will. Clear, that is, to everyone except Bo (short for 'Beauregard'), a gauche and innocent young cowboy who rides into Phoenix, Arizona with his friend Virgil (Arthur O'Connell) on the bus from Montana for a rodeo. He encounters Cherie, for this is the Frenchified name she has chosen to give herself, singing in the Blue Dragon cafe. He thinks she is beautiful, though no one else in the cafe seems to have noticed. Incensed, Bo forces them all to stop talking and listen to Cherie. Touched by his action, Cherie gives him a kiss. Instantly hooked, Bo decides that this beautiful maiden, this wonderful angel

'chantoose' (as she calls herself, her strong Ozarks accent having trouble with the French word *chanteuse*), will be his wife.

Now Cherie is not very bright herself, being convinced to start with that she is made for Sunset Boulevard and better things than being taken off and dumped in the midst of a herd of cattle in Timber Hill, Montana. Also, being vastly more experienced than cowboy Bo, she knows that he would be better off without someone like her. Virgil, too, is unhappy at Bo's decision, since he knows something of Cherie's checkered past.

Bo is not to be deflected from his purpose and the next morning bursts into Cherie's bedroom with the news that they are to be married that very day. Cherie is disbelieving but later, while at the rodeo

Bo makes Cherie's acquaintance: Don Murray and Marilyn Monroe in Bus Stop.

with her waitress friend Vera (Eileen Heckart) she realizes that he does indeed mean what he says and leaves the rodeo in some disorder, heading for the bus station. Virgil, also thinking she would be better out of the way, gives her the money for a ticket to Los Angeles, but before she can leave Bo turns up and herds her off to the bus for Montana. Virgil, despairing, goes with them.

By the time the Montana bus is held up by snow so that it cannot travel beyond a roadside diner, (owned by that splendid actress Betty Field), Cherie has told another passenger, a girl called Elma (Hope Lange) about her plight, and the bus driver Carl (Robert Bray) has also learned of it. When Bo comes along, having noticed that Cherie has taken her case off the bus and put two and two together fast enough to realize that she is planning to flee again, he simply slings her over his shoulder as if she were one of the calves from his herd and stalks off to the nearest preacherman. Carl stops him. There is a fight and Bo is the loser, to his shame and chagrin. The next morning, persuaded by Virgil, Bo apologizes to everyone for his behaviour, including Cherie, who repeats her belief that he will be much better off without her. Bo, preparing to go on to Montana alone now that the road is cleared, gives Cherie one last kiss. Her response, surprising even

Taking the bus to Montana and a happy future: Don Murray as the brash cowboy Bo and Cherie, the girl he has rounded up, in Bus Stop.

A cold stop in the desert for bus passengers Bo and Cherie in Bus Stop.

herself, is such that Bo is encouraged to re-open negotiations until Cherie, in tears, finally agrees to marry him. Virgil, who has come to feel that there is more to Cherie than he had thought, smiles upon them both and stays behind while they head off on the bus towards Montana and a new life together.

As directed by Joshua Logan and acted by its fine cast, *Bus Stop* is a wonderfully warm and human story, a bit rough and raw-boned perhaps, but full of a deeply satisfying combination of comedy and sadness.

The combination is at its finest in Marilyn Monroe's interpretation of Cherie, in which her blending of expertly timed comedy and subtly projected pathos suggested to more than one critic

the skills of Charlie Chaplin. It was not all that difficult for her to suggest the externals of Cherie's character: leave a few sequins hanging off her already tawdry costume, pull holes in the black fishnet tights then sew them together again with clumsy stitches, wear a white, almost clown-like make-up to suggest a washed out and nearly washed-up character, and leave her hair cheaply tinted and unkempt. But the internals, the emotions and psychology of Cherie, who is outwardly just a common floozie, required a very fine judgement indeed on the part of the actress playing her, and Monroe managed it triumphantly. Outstanding among the many fine moments of her performance, is the scene in the cafe where she sings 'That Old Black Magic'. Clad in her cheap

The Actors' Studio was
to benefit from the New
York première of Baby
Doll in December 1956,
so Marilyn went along a
few days beforehand to
launch the sale of tickets
for the occasion.

costume and inexpertly waving a wispy
scarf in the air while with her foot she tries
to find the switches for the stage lighting,
knowing all the while that no one is taking
any notice of her, she comes across as
pathetic, brave, possessed of a certain
pride, and unforgettable.

Some critics, like William Zinsser in the
New York Herald Tribune, said, in effect,
'We told you so: she had the skills, all she
needed was a role with some depth', but
for most, her performance was a revelation. Even crusty Mr. Bosley Crowther in the *New York Times* agreed that at
last Marilyn Monroe in *Bus Stop* finally
proved herself an actress.

Arthur Knight in the *Saturday Review*
considered that in *Bus Stop* Marilyn
Monroe had 'accomplished what is un-
questionably the most difficult feat for any
film personality. She has submerged herself so completely in the role . . . that one
searches in vain for glimpses of the former
calendar girl. It is far more than simply
mastering and maintaining a ludicrous
accent and intonation throughout the
picture . . . . There is pathos, humour, and
a desperate pride about the girl, and Miss
Monroe brings all this to life. Just how
much of it is her own doing can be
surmised from the work of the rest of the
cast . . . . None of them quite manages to
conceal the fact that they are very competently acting out their roles; while Miss
Monroe constantly seems to be living hers
with an emotional range and intensity that
few actresses could duplicate. The real
revelation in *Bus Stop* is Marilyn Monroe, and the incandescence that glows
from the screen the moment she enters the
story'.

Derek Granger, writing in the English
Financial Times, found it still hard to say
how much of her art depended on instinct

or calculation, though 'there is no doubt whatever that her effects go far deeper than those of all her well-built rivals put together. Perhaps this is because her sense of comedy is never wholly divorced from a vulnerable sweetness which lends a sure humanity to almost everything she does'.

The British critics, and many of their fellow countrymen, had had a few rare opportunities to see the actress in the flesh, for by the time *Bus Stop* opened in Britain, Monroe had been there for some months filming *The Prince and the Showgirl* with Laurence Olivier.

She arrived in England in mid-July with a brand new husband, having married Arthur Miller in White Plains, New York, on 29 June 1956, and then again in a Jewish ceremony two days later. Monroe began studying the Jewish faith, which she proposed entering for the sake of her husband, who was Jewish. (Three years later, the United Arab Republic of Egypt and Syria banned all films starring Monroe and Carroll Baker, both of whom were recent converts to Judaism.)

Monroe and Miller had talked about marriage for months, though no specific date had been set, and the actual announcement had surprised her as much as everyone else, for Miller had told the world of his intention to marry her at, of all places, a hearing of the U.S. House Committee on Un-American Activities, before which he had been called to testify about his alleged connections with the Communist Party. Denying that he himself was a member of the Party, Miller steadfastly refused to name other people associated with 'Communist' writers' groups. (For this he would later be cited for contempt of Congress.)

Miller had applied for a passport to visit England later in the summer. Why? asked

Every man's dream? The twentieth century's sexiest blonde casts a 'come hither' look over her furs and sequins.

the Committee. To attend a production of my play in London and to be with the woman who will then be my wife – Marilyn Monroe, replied Miller.

Sensation. The Brain and the Body, the Egghead and the Hourglass (or, alternatively, the Egghead and the Vulture-for-Culture) were going to get married. Rumour was confirmed, and the whole world knew, officially.

The world was still buzzing with excitement when Mr. and Mrs. Miller arrived in London for her to make *The Prince and the Showgirl*, the film which she, at least, saw as the summit of her film career.

The popular press had made sure there was a good lead-up to the arrival. Vivien Leigh, then 42, had announced three days earlier that she was expecting a baby in December and a gentleman of the press had asked if Marilyn Monroe would be a godmother. The Oliviers were taken aback but Sir Laurence managed a tactful reply: 'That's an interesting idea.'

Then the *Daily Express*'s gossip columnist, William Hickey, thought that the nation should know how the nation's main airport proposed coping with the phenomenon due to arrive in a couple

of days and went off to interview officials of the airport and of the Ministry of Civil Aviation. Despite urgent demands for crush barriers and the like from publicity men attending Marilyn, it turned out that the men from the ministry and the airport had no special plans at all. 'We are going to treat it as just another arrival', said a senior official. 'We don't think there will be screaming fans and we don't go in for this publicity ballyhoo. This is London Airport, not Idlewild, New York.' So there!

The publicity men were distraught, according to William Hickey. 'They don't care if Marilyn is crushed by the crowd. This is so important and the whole destiny of the United States and the British Empire might hang on it!'

In fact, the fans turned out to be quite quiet, stunned no doubt by the sight of their goddess. It was the press who got out of hand, stampeding over each other and the tables and chairs in the airport lounge set aside for the first of four huge press conferences Monroe would give during her first three days in England.

It was gruelling, exhausting, and all too soon the ladies and gentlemen of the press

began putting in the needle. Things started off all right – 'She is here. She walks, she talks, she really is as luscious as strawberries and cream', said the *Evening News*. She was photographed drinking English tea, reported to have said that she wanted to play in George Bernard Shaw's 'Pygmalion', that she would now sleep in Yardley's Lavender perfume rather than her usual Chanel No. 5, that she and her husband wanted to live a quiet life in the country and that she would like to ride a bicycle in Windsor Great Park, on the borders of which was the large English country house rented for her stay in England. The *Daily Sketch* sent her a bicycle, then posted a man outside her gate for days waiting for her to appear on it.

But all too soon the press became patronizing, sneering at the girl who liked Beethoven's Symphonies, but could not remember the number of her favourite ('I know it when I hear it') and who could not remember the names of all the so-smart lords and ladies she met at parties ('so wonderful for the little American nobody to meet real aristocrats', went the sneer).

The Millers began keeping themselves to themselves, giving no parties of their own, sheltering behind security men when they went out, refusing invitations for her to play 'Lysistrata' on the B.B.C. Third Programme and for him to appear on The Brains Trust on television. When to this apparent stand-offishness were added stories of difficulties with Olivier, whom Monroe very quickly came to distrust, of rows and disagreements on set and off, of non-appearances by the star, of her inability to remember the simplest line, then the press became actively hostile. She was described as being 'pale and nervous' at the annual Royal Command Film Performance, where she was in the line-up of stars to meet the Queen and Princess Margaret. 'A shocking dress and sloppy hairdo' snorted columnist William Hickey of Monroe's appearance, without too much justification, to judge by the photographs.

It was this dress, worn in typical Monroe style without a girdle, together with stories of sickness that kept her off set, which sparked off rumours that Monroe might be expecting a baby – stories given an added poignancy by the fact that Vivien Leigh had lost her baby in mid-August.

The Millers went back home in November. First, though, Marilyn wrote a letter to the cast and crew of *The Prince*

Movie Queen meets British Queen at the Royal Command Film Performance in London, October 1956. The film was The Battle of the River Plate *and the British press took the opportunity to fire a few shots across Marilyn's bow over the design of her dress, though Queen Elizabeth II does not seem to mind.*

and the Showgirl asking them not to think too badly of her for she really had been ill for much of the shooting. Then there was a final press conference at London Airport.

Tanfield's Diary in the *Daily Mail* reported it with tongue firmly in cheek and metaphorical dagger well between Marilyn Monroe's ribs. 'It was a sacred occasion and conscious of it, we waited humbly', Tanfield began. 'Her departure after four months in England was almost ignored by the public. When she arrived in July, police had to keep the crowds back.' Journalistic licence, this, and carefully ignoring the fact that the weather was cold and the hour late when Marilyn left.

'Mrs. Miller was early. What is more, she was gracious, charming, healthy and fresh as paint.' Tanfield went on to draw a lightning sketch of Paula Strasberg in the background, giving the impression that Marilyn moved when Mrs. Strasberg pulled the strings.

'Mrs. Strasberg smiled again as Marilyn, speaking slowly and carefully – now in the little girl voice of an Elizabeth Bergner – and said: "I do appreciate how good the British people have been to me. I think they are more enthusiastic about me than anyone has been."

'We swallowed bravely and smiled back at the radiantly healthy figure in skin-tight black wool, high-necked dress . . . . Everyone said sweet things about Marilyn, and then about us.

'Before she finally left us Marilyn made a speech in that carefully rehearsed manner. "The biggest thrill for me was meeting your Queen and my husband's new play. But I did have the feeling you

Meeting the press before work begins on The Prince and the Showgirl *are Arthur Miller, Marilyn Monroe, Vivien Leigh and Laurence Olivier.*

British were in the middle of a crisis here. Oh, certainly a crisis."

'We nodded our heads. It was nice to know she had noticed.' (The crisis was, of course, Suez.)

As for *The Prince and the Showgirl*, did it live up to all the ballyhoo, was it worth all the trouble, all the nervous strain and tension? Well, yes and no. It was a thoroughly entertaining film, gorgeous to look at, well acted, elegantly put together. But it was such a trifle, such a piece of marshmallow, that it hardly needed the combined talents of Laurence Olivier and Marilyn Monroe. No matter how good

they were, and neither was brilliant, they could not turn a trifle into a major movie.

The original play, 'The Sleeping Prince' was called by its author, Terence Rattigan, 'an occasional fairytale', written for a specific occasion, the Coronation of Queen Elizabeth II in 1953. Rattigan had envisaged his piece as appearing in the West End during a light-hearted Coronation summer. It would be a pleasant interlude from more serious matters both for audiences and for its stars, the Oliviers. In the event, the play did not reach the stage until late in 1953 where, although the reviews were only moderately good, it enjoyed a successful run. By 1957, when the film version finally appeared, the occasion for Coronation jollities was well past and the background to the story, King George V's Coronation in London in 1911, seemed irrelevant.

The 'Prince' of *The Prince and the Showgirl* is the Grand Duke Charles (Olivier), Prince Regent of Carpathia come to London with his young son King Nicholas (Jeremy Spenser) and his mother-in-law, the Queen Dowager (Sybil Thorndike) to attend the Coronation of George V. The showgirl is a lovely American, Elsie Marina (Monroe), whom the Prince Regent encounters when she joins the line-up of stars after a performance of the show in which she is appearing. The shoulder strap of her dress snaps, the Prince Regent notices and immediately invites her to dinner at the Carpathian Embassy. Innocent Elsie assumes that the occasion is going to be a glittering reception, crowded with elegant and important people. It turns out to be a supper *à deux*, at the end of which Elsie saves her virtue by falling asleep from the effects of too much champagne. She has already met the Prince's mother-in-law, who has taken a fancy to her, and his

Marilyn Monroe as Gay Nineties lovely Lillian Russell. The pose was one of a series of interpretations Monroe did for photographer Richard Avedon and which were published in Life *magazine, whose readers could also view Monroe as Clara Bow, Theda Bara, Jean Harlow and Marlene Dietrich.*

young son who is plotting a palace revolution that will get the power currently held by his father into his own hands.

Next morning, Elsie wakes up to the discovery that she has fallen in love with the Prince, though he clearly does not feel the same for her. Eventually, having attended the Coronation as the bejewelled lady-in-waiting to the Queen Dowager, Elsie manages to reconcile the Prince and his son, thus staving off trouble in Europe, and has won the heart of the Prince.

A slight confection, then, and one that would not have deserved serious critical dissection were it not for the presence of its two great stars. In the end the acting honours were about evenly divided. Many

British critics thought that Olivier had over-acted while Marilyn was a delight; many American critics though that he was wonderful and she was outclassed – left 'ankle-high to such giants of the theatre as her fellow performers, Producer-Director Laurence Olivier and cloud-capped Sybil Thorndike', as *Time* magazine put it.

Perhaps the best summary of the whole thing was the *New York Herald Tribune*'s remark that 'not since Lend-Lease has there been such a stunning example of hands across the sea. . . . They get along fine'. Clearly, the destiny of the United States and the British Empire had not been knocked off course by *The Prince and the Showgirl*.

The Last Films

Once Mr. and Mrs. Arthur Miller were settled back in America, having left the distresses and tensions of filming in England behind them, they had a year and more together free of the hot-house world of film-making in which to put their marriage on a firm foundation. And, from all reports, they were successful, being deeply, totally in love with each other.

Unlike Joe DiMaggio, Arthur Miller did not try to keep out of Marilyn's film-making life, nor did he despise it. Indeed, he turned out to be more supportive of her in her troubles in England than did the vice-president of her production company. When Marilyn's dislike of Laurence Olivier as director and producer of *The Prince and the Showgirl* became intense, she blamed Milton Greene for her troubles, because it was Greene who had set up the arrangement with Olivier. She came to feel that Greene, in having made such a choice, was not to be trusted. Arthur, on the other hand, could be trusted to identify himself with her interests completely.

There was one dark moment, when she found a notebook in which Arthur had been writing comments about the progress of the film which had not been totally in her favour, but on the whole he had been by her side when she needed him. The British newspapers, fed with stories from the closely guarded and locked-up film set by disgruntled crew members angry at Monroe's dismissive treatment of them, reported that Arthur Miller even took Paula Strasberg's place as Marilyn's 'dramatic Svengali' when Olivier dismissed Mrs. Strasberg from the set. 'They are very much in love', wrote Donald Zec of the *Daily Mirror* about the Millers. 'She calls him Popsie Wopsie and he calls her Poopsie Woopsie.

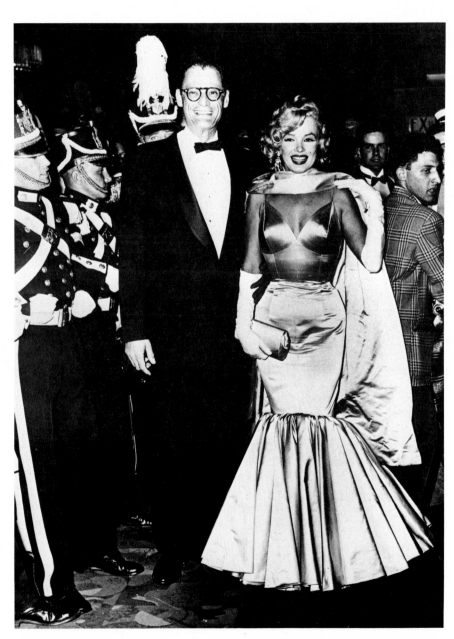

The star and her husband arrive for the New York première of The Prince and the Showgirl, *June 1957.*

So now Marilyn leans on him between takes, visibly and otherwise.'

Back in America, Marilyn was still not feeling like calling Milton Greene by any tender nicknames, and two or three months before *The Prince and the Showgirl* was at last premièred in New York in June 1957, the man who had bought the

Opposite: *Marilyn doing
some charity work in
New York in 1958. She
was helping promote an
anti-polio campaign, the
March of Dimes, at the
Waldorf-Astoria Hotel.*

property for Monroe was forced to sell out his share of Marilyn Monroe Productions Inc. He did leave his mark on her career, however, for some at least of the credit for Elsie Marina's glowing loveliness that lit up *The Prince and the Showgirl* must be attributed to his near-fanatical concern about the way in which Monroe was lit and photographed, while some of the still photographs he took of her are among the finest of them all.

For much of the first half of 1957, America seemed to expect that Monroe's next role would be that of a mother. Wherever the Millers went, there would be sure to be a reporter popping up to ask if she were pregnant. The answer was always 'no comment'. They retired for the summer to a remote part of Long Island, he to carry on with the play he had been working on for some time, she to potter about in the garden, do the shopping, cook meals, to swim in the sea and, apparently, to sunbathe. The latter activity, carried to excess, was given as the reason why the Millers would not be flying the Atlantic to attend the British première of *The Prince and the Showgirl*: she was reported to have burnt her bottom sunbathing in the nude in her Long Island garden. Which must be about the most unlikely excuse ever given for a star's not turning up at a première of her own film. It also does not square with her well-known comment made several years before, that she did not care for a suntan because she liked 'to feel blonde all over'. Still, it was a good story.

By mid-summer, Marilyn Monroe was pregnant. To the great distress of both of them, the pregnancy had to be terminated as it had developed in a Fallopian tube. Her doctors were reported as saying that there was no cause for long-term alarm, as they did not see any reason why she should not conceive again, but she fell into a desperate depression. Arthur Miller, who had always said that he never wrote with any particular person in mind, decided now that he would write a screenplay specifically for his wife. It would be the greatest gift he could give her, an expression of his devotion just as Richard Wagner's 'Siegfried Idyll' had been for his wife. He chose to adapt a short story he had written called 'The Misfits' which had been published in *Esquire*.

In the meantime, it also seemed a good idea that Marilyn should get back to work, rather than sit brooding. Billy Wilder had written asking her to consider a part in a film he had had in mind for some time, a comedy set in the Prohibition Era in which she could play – yet again – a singer with a troubled romantic past, a role that would be part comedy, part sadness. There would also be a couple of men dressed as women playing major roles. Wilder felt that his idea might work best as a film if the female lead was played by Monroe, whose unique blend of sex and innocence would help to forestall the distaste audiences might feel at the sight ot two men in drag for an entire movie. In the event, his own tight direction and the script ensured there was no such feeling; audiences were always aware that these were two men constantly chaffing against their female attire and the deception they were forced to play.

Persuaded by her husband, Monroe agreed to play in *Some Like It Hot*. She got top billing even though her part had considerably less weight than those of the two men, and thus found herself in one of the wildest, funniest and most successful films ever made. It was certainly the greatest hit of Wilder's not unsuccessful career, and probably of Monroe's, too, for of all her films it is the one which, twenty years after her death, is probably revived most often on television and in specialist film houses all over the world.

Some Like It Hot tells the story of two jazz musicians, Joe (Tony Curtis) and Jerry (Jack Lemmon) who inadvertently see a gangland murder while working in Chicago in 1929. They are the only witnesses when Spats Colombo (George Raft) and his gang massacre a rival mob in a garage. Unfortunately, they are spotted before they can get away, Jerry's double bass is riddled with bullets, and the two have to go into hiding, fast.

They make their getaway from Chicago by dressing as women and joining an all-female band, Sweet Sue's Society Syncopaters, which has an engagement way down in Florida, far enough away, Joe and Jerry reckon, for them to be safe from the Chicago Mobsters.

The band's lead singer and ukelele player is a lovely lady with a penchant for liquor, which she keeps in a flask tucked

under her garter, and also for millionaires. She is Sugar Kane (Monroe) and very soon Joe (now calling himself Josephine) is deeply attracted to her. There is a long train ride ahead of them down to the warm south in which they can become better acquainted. Jerry, renamed Daphne, also becomes well acquainted with the members of the band when a dozen or so of them climb into his/her top berth for a merry drinking party. (This zany scene recalls so vividly that wildly chaotic scene in the shipboard stateroom in the Marx Brothers' *A Night at the Opera* that the viewer is in constant expectation of someone calling out 'Make that three hard boiled eggs'.)

Once down in sunny Florida, where the welcoming song is 'Down Among the Sheltering Palms' and the geriatric millionaires are laid out in wheelchaired rows on the hotel terrace, Josephine and Daphne settle down to life with the band and generally trying to live the lives of true females. During one of the band's rehearsals Daphne takes responsibility for Sugar's flask to save her from the wrath of bandleader Sweet Sue (Joan Shawlee), who has already warned her about her tippling.

Jerry's pose as Daphne is so successful, outwardly anyway, that 'she' attracts the keen interest of millionaire Osgood Fielding III (Joe E. Brown), who owns a large

Right: *Sweet Sue's Society Syncopaters rehearse on the train to Florida, with Josephine (Tony Curtis), Daphne (Jack Lemmon) and Sugar (Marilyn Monroe) among the musicians – a scene from* Some Like It Hot *(1959).*

Opposite: *The top berth is filling up fast. On the Florida train in* Some Like It Hot.

Opposite: *Sugar on the beach in* Some Like It Hot.

Right: *Heading for a millionaire's yacht and a night of romance.*

yacht moored in the harbour. Joe persuades Jerry/Daphne to encourage Osgood in his advances on shore so that he can use the yacht as part of his plan to seduce Sugar by letting her think he is a millionaire, to which end he has already acquired a yachting cap, a blazer and a wonderful Cary Grant accent. He has led Sugar to believe (by waving a shell from the beach in front of her) that the source of his wealth is a large and not unknown oil company and also that he is a shy lad with a complex about women so great that he is unable to get excited about them. Sugar, determined to cure him of his complex, willingly accompanies him in a small motorboat to the yacht – backwards, since poor Joe is unable to master the engine.

Meanwhile, back on shore, Daphne, a rose between her teeth, is dancing a spirited tango with Osgood, by now totally taken up with her charms, even though she will insist on leading when they dance. Joe returns from the yacht to find Jerry, still in female attire, lying on his bed, shaking a pair of maracas and intoning 'I'm engaged, I'm engaged.'

But trouble and the threat of being shot

full of more holes than Jerry's double-bass is suddenly all too horribly close again. The hotel's convention for 'Friends of Italian Opera' turns out to be a cover for a gangland get-together, including Spats Colombo and his gang. Joe and Jerry, on the run again, take cover under the heavily draped tables in the 'convention' room and are thus witnesses to a second gangland massacre, this time of Spats and his boys, gunned down by a man who leaps out of a birthday cake with a machine-gun in his hands. Although the policeman (Pat O'Brien), who has been on the gangsters' trail bursts in, demanding the recipe for the cake that did not agree with Spats, he is unable to prevent the second gang of killers giving chase after Joe and Jerry, who decide that their only hope is Osgood's motorboat. While Jerry is looking for Osgood, Joe, who has already telephoned Sugar to say goodbye, hears Sugar singing in the hotel ballroom, with moving poignancy, 'I'm Through with Love'. Joe rushes on stage and, still in his Josephine clothes, kisses her, saying that no man is worth such distress.

As he and Jerry are leaving in the motorboat, Osgood at the wheel, Sugar comes flying down to the harbour on a bicycle. She knows that Joe is a far-from-rich impostor, but she had decided that he is the man for her, so she jumps into the boat with them. Which leaves only Osgood to be put in the picture. Daphne starts slowly, saying she would be no good as a marriage partner: 'I smoke . . . I can never have children.' Osgood shrugs, untroubled. Desperate, Jerry pulls off Daphne's wig and says 'I'm a man!'. Osgood, mildly surprised, continues driving and says 'Well, nobody's perfect'.

Based on a story by R. Thoxeren and M. Logan, the *Some Like It Hot* screenplay was written by Billy Wilder and I.A.L. Diamond, who was to collaborate with Wilder on several very successful films, including *The Apartment*. Their witty, sophisticated and perceptive screenplay was the essential basis for the success of the film, which was directed and acted with a lively exuberance and a joyous and surprisingly innocent optimism that negated what should have been the horror of the two gangland shootings and the desperation of Joe's and Jerry's position.

The film's finely drawn evocation of time and place, also helped give it a strong structure. This was due partly to Billy Wilder's near-infallible attention to detail and partly to his decision to make the film in black and white. Monroe had wanted colour but Wilder had persuaded her that the film, and Tony Curtis's and Jack Lemmon's parts in it, would look more believable in mono. Apart from making the two actors' heavy female make-up acceptable to audiences (it had looked appalling in colour), the use of black and white also gave the film a beautifully nostalgic period flavour: this was indeed the long-lost age of jazz and prohibition, recreated for audiences of the late 1950s, in a style that recalled numerous periods of film comedy, especially the slapstick of the silent era and the Marx Brothers' films of the 1930s.

The wonderfully spontaneous air in *Some Like It Hot* seems all the more miraculous considering the troubles Wilder and the rest of the cast had with Marilyn. Indeed, Wilder is reported to have said that he deserved some sort of medal – like a Purple Heart – for directing *two* films with her.

She was, in fact, hell to work with. All the troubles of lateness and sickness that had bedevilled *The Prince and the Showgirl*, during the filming of which Paula Strasberg was reported as standing on the sidelines ready to dish out pills to Marilyn at regular intervals, were exaggerated a hundredfold on the set of *Some Like It Hot*. She seemed unable on occasions to say the simplest, three-word sentence, set-ups would need anything up to four or five dozen takes to get acceptably on to film, and she would keep actors and film crew waiting about for hours until she deigned to appear. She was rude to the sound stage crew, she sometimes even ignored Billy Wilder. Towards the end of filming, the latter part of 1958, she became pregnant again, and her natural concern that all should be well this time probably affected her work, too. In the event, she also lost this baby, in December. A few months later she would have a minor gynaecological operation which it was hoped would make pregnancy surer.

None of these troubles affected the finished product. *Some Like It Hot* was an instant success – everywhere, and in a

159

dozen languages. If the critics, especially outside America, had initial reservations about what they saw as its vulgarity, audiences everywhere showed no such inhibitions and the film was a big money-spinner for Mirisch Productions and United Artists from the time it was released. Marilyn herself garnered some fine reviews. Given the revealing nature of most of her costumes in *Some Like It Hot*, at least two of which looked as if they were being precariously held up by gravity and her nipples, it is not surprising that her physical charms were remarked on at length, but many critics retained sufficient balance of judgement to be able to notice her acting skills as well. Said *Variety*, 'She is a comedienne with that combination of sex appeal and timing that just can't be beat', while for Archer

Winsten in the *New York Post*, 'Marilyn does herself proud'. *Time* magazine, on the other hand, while enjoying the film, thought that Marilyn had been 'trimmer, slimmer and sexier in earlier films'.

Over in Britain, where society was perhaps still rather more prim in its outlook than in America, *Some Like It Hot* proved a little more hard to swallow. Miss C.A. Lejeune, the *Observer*'s critic, for instance, found the 'mixture of machine-gun bloodbath and female impersonation so intolerable and the jokes about physical geography so wearisome' that she left by a side exit before the end, and the *People*'s critic found two hours of 'that most be-whiskered of all gags, female imperson-ation, a high price to pay for a couple of songs from Marilyn'. Well, at least he liked her singing, which was indeed

Tony Curtis, director Billy Wilder and Marilyn Monroe in conversation during a press reception for Some Like It Hot.

Philippe Halsman contended you could assess people's characters from the way they jumped up and down, and took a series of photos in 1959 to prove it. What to make of Marilyn Monroe's generous smile and clenched hands?

memorable, in her usual evocatively sexy and little-girl whispery style. She sang three songs, 'I'm Through With Love' by Gus Kahn, Matty Malneck and F. Livingston; 'Running Wild' by Joe Gray and Leo Worth and 'I Wanna Be Loved by You' by Bert Kalmar, Harry Ruby and Herbert Stothart.

A more balanced review came from Dilys Powell in the *Sunday Times*, who told her readers they would not be wasting their time by seeing *Some Like It Hot*, which was 'brisked up by moments of savagery and enjoyable bad taste . . . Most of the time Billy Wilder's new piece – a farce blacker than is common on the American screen – whistles along at a smart, murderous pace . . . Tony Curtis, whom one used to think of as simply a haircut, gets better and better. A touch of the ridiculous, sweeter, perhaps, but not cloying, is provided by Marilyn Monroe, both physically and spiritually at her ooziest.' When the film was re-released in Britain eight years later, the critics were almost unanimous in declaring that it was a brilliant, classic comedy.

Some Like It Hot had been completed by the end of 1958 and was released in February 1959. The Millers both attended the première, she in a dress reported to be so tight 'there was hardly room for her skin in there, let alone underwear'. Very long earrings and a white fur completed her ensemble. He completed his outfit of tuxedo and black tie with a rather shapeless felt hat. They were an hour late.

Monroe did not work on another film until 1960. This time, she went back to Twentieth Century-Fox, for only the second film for them under the 1956 contract. The film was *Let's Make Love* and it and the man chosen to play opposite Monroe, Italian-born French actor and singer Yves Montand, were to help lift Marilyn out of her depression over the loss of her second baby. The press had already noted Marilyn Monroe's interest in Montand, having reported some time previously that her 'favourite Broadway show is a two-hour programme by French singer Yves Montand. She has seen it three times in two weeks'.

Fox had had trouble casting the lead male role in *Let's Make Love*. Gregory Peck was said to have pulled out when Arthur Miller's rewriting of the original

Norman Krasna screenplay had reduced the role, and other Hollywood stars had been lukewarm. Eventually Monroe herself suggested Montand. The Millers' interest in him was natural enough. He was a good and experienced film actor, having made his mark in the early 1950s in the Clouzot-directed thriller, *La Salaire de la Peur* (*Wages of Fear*), and he and his wife, Simone Signoret, had starred in a French film version of Arthur Miller's *The Crucible* in 1957.

Meeting the press before filming started on Let's Make Love *(1960) are Arthur Miller, French actress Simone Signoret, her husband Yves Montand, Marilyn Monroe and Frankie Vaughan.*

If it was natural enough that the Millers and the Montands should find interest and pleasure in each other's company, it was probably natural enough too that the gossip columnists of the world should take a considerable interest in the relationship between Mrs. Miller and Mr. Montand when their respective spouses left them alone in each other's company in Hollywood. Arthur was spending as much time in New York and in Ireland (where he was having meetings with John Huston

over *The Misfits*) as in Hollywood and Simone Signoret had to go back to Europe to make a film, so there seemed nothing to prevent Marilyn and Yves keeping close company off the set as well as on.

Although Marilyn always replied to importunate reporters that she was not having an affair with Montand, who 'is a married man', there was no doubt in anyone's mind that she was very much attracted to him – she even told the press that she thought him, next to her husband

and alongside Marlon Brando, the most attractive man she had ever met. For her part, Simone Signoret was more than somewhat troubled by all the gossip. Arthur Miller, still trying to make something of the banal script of *Let's Make Love*, must have been indescribably hurt to realize that Montand had lifted Marilyn out of her depression more successfully than he could. By the time *Let's Make Love* was completed, things had started to go badly wrong for the Miller marriage.

Maybe Twentieth Century-Fox were not all that troubled by all the publicity about an apparently tempestuous affair going on between their expensive sex goddess and the French singer/actor. *Let's Make Love* was not much of a film, being a lightweight romance with some music and dancing, and it was clearly going to need all the publicity it could get.

Let's Make Love is another backstage story, this time about an off-Broadway theatrical group about to put on a satirical revue, one of the targets of which will be a prominent millionaire, Jean-Marc Clement (Montand), head of Clement Enterprises. Having been told by his lawyer John Wales (Wilfred Hyde White) and public relations chief, Alex Coffman

Opposite: *The warm and lovely star of* Let's Make Love.

Left: *Marilyn Monroe, Gene Kelly and Yves Montand on the set of* Let's Make Love.

Overleaf: *Monroe and Montand find an opportunity to be romantic in* Let's Make Love.

(Tony Randall) that he is about to become the butt of this company, Clement takes himself off, incognito, to find out what is going on.

Once at the theatre, he is immediately attracted to the company's singer, Amanda Dell (Monroe) whom he encounters rehearsing one of her songs, while the show's director, noticing the resemblance, thinks he is a natural for the part of Jean-Marc Clement in the revue. The real Clement agrees to take the part because it will allow him to be near Amanda. At first, he seems to make little headway with her as she seems more interested in the show's male singer and comic, Tony Danton (Frankie Vaughan).

Clement takes his new role of song-and-dance man very seriously, and arranges for three celebrities (guest parts for Bing Crosby, Gene Kelly and Milton Berle) to teach him the basics of song, dance and comedy. In the meantime Clement Enterprises, which turns out to own the theatre, is planning to close it down – a move that so annoys P.R.-man Coffman, that, fortified with Dutch courage from a bottle, he tells his employer off in fierce

Giving a boost to the Aran knitwear industry, Marilyn signs Cole Porter's 'My Heart Belongs to Daddy' in Let's Make Love.

language. Clement, so far from wanting to close down the show that is proposing to satirize him, has decided to turn theatrical angel and put money into it. His lawyer, Wales, is put up as a front for Clement, pretending to be the backer himself.

Engineered by Amanda into taking her out to dinner Clement takes the opportunity to confess that he is not really a budding singer but the billionaire head of Clement Enterprises and he also asks her to marry him. Amanda does not believe him, and also turns down his proposal.

Still in pursuit of Amanda, Clement tries the clever trick of taking out an injunction to stop the show going ahead, and then manoeuvres Amanda into taking him, under his guise as a fellow cast member, along with her when she goes to try to persuade the theatre's owner to lift his injunction so that the show can go on. In the end, of course, Amanda finds out

who Clement really is, realizes that she loves him and falls into his arms in a tender embrace.

Just as *Let's Make Love* was far from being the most exciting musical Fox had ever turned out, so Monroe's part in it was hardly one to inspire confidence in the studio's belief in her capabilities. The part was shallow, cardboard, her lines were totally unmemorable and there was little for her to do except look beautiful and desirable and to sing four songs, all of which she did very nicely indeed, but her abilities were left unstretched. Three of her songs were by Sammy Cahn and James Van Heusen: 'Let's Make Love,' 'Incurably Romantic' and 'Specialization', and there was one big production number, Cole Porter's 'My Heart Belongs to Daddy', which she sang and danced as if in rehearsal, wearing sheer black leotard and a thick Aran-knit sweater. Jack Cole,

Charlton Heston, Marilyn Monroe and Rock Hudson at the 1960 Golden Globe Awards ceremony.

with whom Marilyn had worked so well for *Gentlemen Prefer Blondes*, did the choreography, and it worked splendidly – a wonderfully exuberant number.

Arthur Miller, like Paula Strasberg, was on set for as much of the filming as he could attend between trips to New York and Ireland. Much to director George Cukor's fury, he often also sat through the rushes, offering comments and opinions. George Cukor had over a long career shown considerable skill in handling difficult female stars and no doubt felt he should have been left alone to handle Monroe. As it happened she did not behave at all badly during this film, apart from the inevitable latenesses, and she also worked very hard, especially on her musical numbers, so that it is surprising that Cukor did not get a particularly scintillating performance out of her. Perhaps his opinion of her – he was once quoted as saying she was mad, subject to bad advice and beyond the reach of communication – prevented him seeing beyond the difficult lady to the gifted actress inside.

Let's Make Love opened to favourable reviews on the whole, critics considering it an entertaining show, fine for passing a pleasant evening in the cinema. There was a mixed bag of reviews for the main players. Many critics thought Marilyn did not have a part that allowed her to do justice to her talents. Said Brendan Gill in the *New Yorker*: 'The supposed star of *Let's Make Love* is Marilyn Monroe, and it's sad to report that although she works as hard as ever, she doesn't accomplish very much this time. Some of the blame is hers – what the *Tribune* has peculiarly called her "flare for comedy" is more of a flicker than a flare, and Mr. Cukor has been unable to draw from her what Billy Wilder drew in *Some Like It Hot* – but most of the blame lies with the script, which is an elaborate nonsense.'

Mr. Gill reserved his praises for Yves Montand, 'a performer of extraordinary charm and intelligence. If playing the romantic lead in a picture as big and many-colored and empty as the Grand Canyon has left M. Montand unscathed, what wonders could he not perform in a trifle, modestly written and directed?'

It was an opinion shared by Leonard Mosley in Britain's *Daily Express* who headed his review of the film 'The eclipse of Marilyn Monroe'. Not, he hastened to add, that Miss Monroe had lost 'that old rumpty-tumpty, as someone once described her particular charm. She is still as blonde and goo-eyed as ever. She still puckers her lips, sings in a childish treble and acts like a little girl lost looking for a skirt which some cad has torn off her. And she certainly has not got any *thinner*, if you know what I mean.

'But she does have the film stolen from under her pretty rabbit-nose by one of the best ferrets in the business – a Frenchman by the name of Yves Montand. His achievement is considerable . . . he pulls off the picture snatch of the decade.'

Mr. Clancy Sigal, in *Time and Tide*, did not agree. 'Monroe, Monroe all the way', he said. 'I admit I am a late-comer to the society of Monroe admirers. . . . But I see now that they are right. She is much of what they say, an orphan goddess of sex, an immensely skilled, if narrowly talented, player lushly clattering up and down the vertebrae of our sexual spines. In this picture . . . Monroe emerges as what she must always have been, the true, satire successor to Mae West.'

Time magazine, saying that Montand seemed restrained by his part, also kept most of its praise for Monroe. 'There is a lot of Marilyn to admire these days, but it is still in fine fettle; at 34 she makes 21 look ridiculous. The smile that reassures nervous males ("It's all right, I'm not real") has never been more dazzling. And the comic counter-point of fleshy grandeur and early Shirley Temple manner is better than ever.'

From *Let's Make Love* Marilyn went more or less straight into work on *The Misfits* which began shooting in Nevada in July 1960. The director, John Huston, had first seen Arthur Miller's script in 1958 when the playwright had sent it to him on the advice of his friend, the publisher and film producer, Frank Taylor. Huston was impressed from the outset, as was Clark Gable when he read it. Montgomery Clift and Eli Wallach were also quickly lined up for the film, but it would be nearly two years before everyone was free of other commitments and able to start work.

Arthur Miller's original story had not had a part for Marilyn Monroe, being a

Photo call for The Misfits *(1960). In front are Montgomery Clift, Marilyn and Clark Gable; behind are Eli Wallach, Arthur Miller and John Huston.*

story about three cowboys who captured misfit horses for sale to dog-food canners. When he decided to write a screenplay geared specifically to his wife's unique talents, he built up a minor female character into a major part, whose interactions with the three men gave a new dimension to the original story. John Huston, in conversation with Arthur Miller and the British journalist, W.J. Weatherby, in Ireland, summed up *The Misfits* as being about people 'who aren't willing to sell their lives. They will sell their work but they won't sell their lives and for that

reason they are misfits.' He saw the film as being about a world in a state of change, and change for the worse, a 'dogs-eat-horse society'. He also saw it as a major work which he expected to be a box-office success. By the time filming was completed, on what was at that time one of the most costly black-and-white movies ever made, he could even see great Oscar-winning potential in Clark Gable's superb performance.

In *The Misfits*, Marilyn Monroe plays Roslyn Taber, a New York woman, sophisticated, sexually free and in a state of emotional turmoil, who comes to Reno, Nevada, to get a divorce from her husand (a small part in the film for Kevin McCarthy). She takes a room in a boarding house where the landlady (Thelma Ritter) introduces her to a cowboy, Guido (Eli Wallach) who is also a sad man, knocked off his emotional balance by the death of his wife.

Guido, attracted to Roslyn, makes the mistake of introducing her to Gay Langland (Clark Gable), a rugged and aging but still very attractive cowboy. Soon, Roslyn and Gay are in love. She is attracted to him for his individualism and self-sufficiency, perhaps best demonstrated in a scene where the drunk Gay, having missed a meeting with his two children first weeps against a car in the street, but then pulls himself together accepting himself for what he is.

Gay has his eye on a herd of wild mustangs which he wants to capture to sell for slaughter and persuades Guido and a rodeo rider called Perce Howland (Montgomery Clift) to join him in the round-up. That Howland is past his best as a rodeo rider becomes clear when he is seen in action at a local rodeo, where he is quite badly hurt.

Roslyn also goes along for the round-up, but is deeply shocked when she realizes that the beautiful animals are to be converted into dog-food. There follows a scene of great emotional and physical violence as Roslyn, having failed in her attempt to make Gay call off the round-up, persuades Perce to release the horses already caught. Gay, enraged, recaptures the most important horse after a struggle which has him at times being dragged across the ground by the struggling wild animal. Having proved his dominance over both horse and man, Gay lets the animal go.

Since the round-up has been a failure, the team splits up, the men go their own way, each having learned something about his own character from the episode. Roslyn Taber and Gay Langland go off together to try to make a new start.

Despite Monroe's powerful female presence, *The Misfits* in John Huston's hands becomes very much a study of the male character, of men dependent on and needing the love of a woman and yet

Clark Gable and Marilyn Monroe in The Misfits.

Sharing a concern for captured horses: Marilyn and Monty in The Misfits.

Opposite: *Gable and Monroe find a shady place in* The Misfits.

strong enough, all three of them, to be able to face death without fear, accepting it as inevitable. As Gay Langland said, 'We've all got to go sometime, dying's as natural as living. A man who's afraid to die is afraid to live'. Doubly ironic words, these, for Gable was to suffer a heart attack and die in November 1960 within weeks of finishing his part in the film. He gave one of the best performances of his long career in *The Misfits*, interpreting the part of Gay Langland, finely drawn by Arthur Miller, with a wonderful subtlety.

Monroe produced a more than adequate account of the character of Roslyn despite the fact that no one could ever call John Huston a woman's director, able to draw from an actress, or perhaps even conceive, a performance of feminine ten-derness or sexual response. Throughout *The Misfits* Monroe was also working against the emotional storms of her own nature, compounded by the knowledge that her marriage to the man she had once admired and respected before all others was breaking up and beyond help.

She no longer respected him, no longer had faith in his abilities, perhaps even found him without masculine strength, in contrast to, say, Clark Gable, who had figured in her mind since childhood as the epitome of male beauty and dependability. She may, too, have known instinctively that the character Arthur Miller had written for her had less strength, less reality than that of Gay. There were stories of bitter arguments between Monroe and Miller over the way

her part was written. According to their good friend, writer and poet Norman Rosten, whose wife had acted as Marilyn's secretary/companion on the trip to England in 1956, when the Miller-Monroe marriage had been new and beautiful, Marilyn's 'hero', Arthur Miller, had by the time of *The Misfits*, 'become the "enemy" – a representative of the movie industry, using her much the same way as the others. The husband/protector was no longer there: they were now involved in a business arrangement.'

In this, her last film, Monroe's problems of nervousness, lack of confidence and sheer terror of film-making reached a dreadful climax. With Paula Strasberg constantly at her side, and Arthur Miller pushed relentlessly into the background, Monroe reached such a state of drug

dependence that there were mornings when she could not speak coherently enough to be able to do a scene. There were whole days when she did not appear at all, many more when Huston got only an afternoon's work out of her.

By August, work had become impossible for her, and she entered a private hospital in Los Angeles where her analyst and the medical staff were able to get her off the barbiturates she had been taking in huge doses. She did not return to Nevada until late in September, by which time the film's schedule was hopelessly awry. It would be late in October before the cast and crew of *The Misfits* could leave the exhausting heat of the Nevada desert.

Given such nightmarish conditions, it is a miracle that Monroe turned in the performance she did: a miraculous triumph of a will which was stronger than all her doubts and fears.

When *The Misfits* was released in February 1961, it received mixed, though by no means unfavourable reviews. Many critics found it impossible to separate the theme and story of *The Misfits* from the real-life story of the Monroe-Miller marriage. Many also found it impossible to work out the meaning of Arthur Miller's screenplay – so serious were the film's literary pretensions that many of the reviewers didn't attempt to look deeper than the surface of the story.

Not so *Time* magazine, whose critic had a good stab at summing it up. '*The Misfits* is a dozen pictures rolled into one. Most of them, unfortunately, are terrible. . . . It is . . . an honest but clumsy western, a pseudosociological study of the American cowboy in the last, disgusting stages of obsolescence, a raucous ode to Reno and the horrors of divorce, a ponderous disquisition on man's inhumanity to man, woman and various animals, an obtuse attempt to write sophisticated comedy, a woolly lament for the loss of innocence in American life and, above all, a glum, long (2 hr 5 min) fatuously embarrassing psychoanalysis of Marilyn Monroe, Arthur Miller and what went wrong with their famous marriage.' Finding most of the picture, despite Huston's skilful directing, 'rambling, banal, loaded with logy [*sic*] profundities', *Time* had nothing to tell its readers about the quality of the acting.

Below: A rare event during the filming of The Misfits*: Marilyn Monroe manages a carefree smile for photographer Eve Arnold.*

For *The Guardian*'s film critic, it was not Monroe's acting which bothered him so much as her role, which he felt 'will not do'. 'We all accept that these men should adore her . . . she is nothing if not lovely. But what is too much to take is that so pathetic a creature as she plays should be glorified into a kind of life force. If symbolism is, indeed, intended then she must be meant to be most symbolic of all; but, in fact, her role just cannot carry so big a burden of significance – it really expresses no more than a neurotic individuality and symbolises little . . .'

A review that did give considerable thought to the quality of the acting was that published in *The Times*, whose critic, doubtful about the ability of the slight tale of *The Misfits* to carry the great weight of significance loaded on it, had no doubts about the cast. 'Clark Gable, in his last film role, plays with effortless ease and authority. . . . But above all, Miss Marilyn Monroe, given a completely impossible part to play, makes it credible, if hardly likeable, by the sheer strength of her own passionate identification with the character. Considerations of whether she can really act seem as irrelevant as they were with Garbo; it is her rare gift just to *be* in front of the camera.'

The formal announcement of the end of Marilyn Monroe's marriage to Arthur Miller was made in November 1960, soon after filming on *The Misfits* was finished. A couple of weeks later, Clark Gable died and Monroe felt bereft, for she had developed a real friendship with him during the making of *The Misfits*. She had discovered him to be a real gentleman, a man of thoughtfulness and consideration, and when the gossip columnists suggested that the difficulties she had caused on the set may have hastened his heart attack, she was deeply distressed.

Marilyn Monroe went to Mexico, quietly, without fuss, to get her divorce from Arthur Miller, who not long afterwards married *Magnum* photographer Inge Morath, who had been among the huge posse of press people covering the filming of *The Misfits* in Nevada.

Now Joe DiMaggio came back into Marilyn's life: fine, dependable Joe who was probably more suited to being the big brother she had never had, than her husband. In January 1961 he was reported as escorting her to the theatre in New York to see Brendan Behan's play 'The Hostage.'

What the papers did *not* report was his rescuing her from a New York psychiatric hospital in February 1961. Despairing of her depressed mental state, her doctor had

Close-up portrait by Eve Arnold.

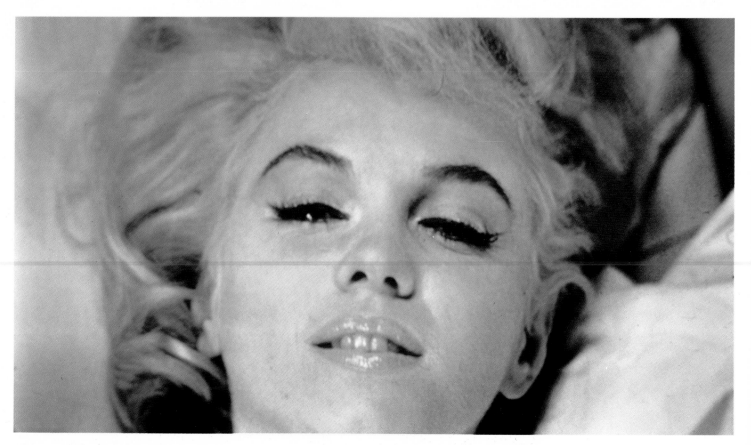

The nude bathing scene from the unfinished Something's Got to Give.

put her in the Payne-Whitney Clinic for treatment without telling her it was a psychiatric hospital. When she discovered she was in a closed room with her day clothing taken away, she was, not unnaturally, distraught and called to Joe for help. He flew straight from Florida, got her out of the clinic via a back door and into another hospital, the Columbia Presbyterian Medical Centre, where she agreed to stay for treatment. The newspapers reported that her stay in the Columbia hospital was to be 'a short rest' for the 34-year-old actress who was suffering from 'insomnia and emotional exhaustion'. Some went further and said that 'her friends are worried. During the past few weeks she has sought more and more consolation from sleeping pills'. Others ran articles with titles like 'The Golden Goddess who cracked'. They also noticed that she had been seeing a woman psychiatrist regularly in New York.

The gossip about the mental state of Marilyn Monroe went around the world, and when she finally left the hospital early in March there were fifty photographers and reporters waiting outside, along with a crowd of about 300 fans. She gave them a good show: her hair looked blonde and well cared-for, her make-up was perfect, and her smile was dazzling. It was also announced that her next role would be Sadie Thompson in a television production of *Rain* to be directed by Lee Strasberg. It was a part the studio should have thought of instead of putting her in *Let's Make Love*. Everyone said she would be starting work soon. It looked as if the Marilyn Monroe career was going to carry on as if she had not a care in the world.

She herself was next seen down in St. Petersburg, Florida, accompanying Joe to the baseball training field where he was acting as unpaid coach to the Yankees. She even took part in the training, just for the fun of it. Eventually, she left New York and the Actors' Studio and returned to Hollywood, buying a Mexican-style house hardly more than a mile or two from where she had been born.

She had a new analyst, Dr. Ralph Greenson, who allowed his patient to enter into the home life of his family, she was going out on dates again, notably with Frank Sinatra, and she had also, around this time, made contact again with her elder half-sister, Berneice Miracle, one of Gladys's two children by her first marriage. Marilyn was to see quite a lot of this lost relative, and thought enough of her to make her a beneficiary of her will.

In the spring of 1962, Monroe started work on a new film for Twentieth Century-Fox. Its title, the dreadful irony of which has escaped no one writing about Marilyn Monroe, was *Something's Got to Give*. It was to be another light-hearted –

Marilyn well wrapped up after filming the swimming pool sequence for Something's Got to Give.

that is to say, banal – story directed by George Cukor, in which she was teamed up with Dean Martin, Cyd Charisse, and Phil Silvers. From the start, Marilyn's lateness on set, her problems of communication with director, actors and others on the set, her inability to learn the script, bedevilled the production. In the few minutes of film that were obtained, Marilyn, looking as beautiful as ever, is seen naked in a swimming pool.

The studio's patience was wearing very thin. When she was sensationally disobedient enough to leave Hollywood in May to fly to New York to sing 'Happy Birthday' to President Kennedy at a Madison Square Garden party (to which she was escorted by her ex-father-in-law, Isidore Miller), it snapped. The front office was not beguiled by the pictures of their most expensive property, clad in a dress which clung to her like a sparkling cobweb of sequins and glittering stones, singing 'Happy Birthday' before 20,000 guests and the President of the United States in a way it had never been sung before. The President might say, with a broad smile, he could now retire from politics, but the moguls of Twentieth Century-Fox were not smiling. Even the nude swimming-pool scenes failed to impress them, and on 7 June 1962, they fired her for 'wilful violation' of her contract. Fox had been put to enough expense with that great fiasco *Cleopatra*, starring Elizabeth Taylor, to be prepared to risk any more on Marilyn Monroe. They even indicated that they were going to try to get back what she had cost them over the years by slapping a $500,000 law suit on Marilyn Monroe Productions Inc.

She never quite gave up the struggle over the next two months. Other film offers came flooding in, and she had hopes that the studio might change their minds and start the cameras rolling again on *Something's Got to Give*. On 4 August, she rang her good friend Norman Rosten in New York, making a date with him and his wife for September, when she was planning to come east again. 'We'll have a great time. We have to start living again, right?', she said.

The next night, she went to bed, took an overdose from her copious supplies of barbiturates and, some time during the night of 5/6 August 1962, she died.

Marilyn's last, and
certainly not her best,
cheesecake pose: a
publicity still for
Something's Got to
Give.

How Real
Is the Legend?

The point about legends is that they are not real. On the other hand, somewhere, however far back beyond the horizon of real life, there has to be some historic truth on which to base a legend.

In the case of Marilyn Monroe the truth was obscured by her own view of what it was good and proper to tell people, and by the fact that she had had a childhood so insecurely based that its reality was hard to find anyway. Add to this the fact that her role in life, her film star status, made it inevitable that the amount of true things known about her would be tailored by film studio publicists, re-written by gossip columnists, and whispered over dinner tables and barroom drinks by 'friends' and enemies, each with his or her own view of the subject to promote, and you are left with a 'truth' not easy to come at.

The sensational circumstances surrounding her death also ensured that her life story should become a legend. Not that there was anything sensational about the death itself. As far as we know she simply said 'Goodnight' to her housekeeper and secretary, went to her bedroom, made a few telephone calls, took more pills than were necessary just to get some sleep, perhaps made one or two more phone calls, then died.

Or maybe she did not.

Since the early 1970s, the rumour has been current that Marilyn Monroe's overdose of barbiturates was inflicted upon her by someone else, someone in the pay of, or working on the orders of, the F.B.I. or the C.I.A. Whole books have been published on the theory that Marilyn Monroe was murdered. Tony Sciacca's 'Who Killed Marilyn? (And Did the Kennedys Know?)' is one such.

The alleged F.B.I. involvement rested on the theory that someone wanted to incriminate the then Attorney General, Robert Kennedy, in a scandal that would lose him, and perhaps the Democrats, their offices. The suggestion that Monroe was killed to stop her talking about C.I.A.

plots to murder Cuba's Fidel Castro has been taken more seriously since other stories about C.I.A. plans to do just that have leaked out of U.S. government circles.

The rumours were investigated over a ten-year period by a Los Angeles private detective, Milo Speriglio, who claimed that Monroe had a romance with President John Kennedy, followed by a more serious affair with Robert Kennedy, which ended just before she died. Much has also been made of a detailed 'red diary' that Monroe is supposed to have kept during the last months of her life and which was said to have fallen into Speriglio's hands, but neither it nor its contents have ever been shown publicly.

The Los Angeles district attorney car-ried out a five-months-long investigation into these allegations, announcing in December 1982 that, in his view, Marilyn Monroe had not been murdered. An affair with Robert Kennedy has also been vigorously denied by those close to her, including Norman Rosten and actor Peter Lawford, the Kennedys' brother-in-law, at whose house Monroe did meet Robert Kennedy on more than one occasion.

The other 'murderer' of Marilyn Monroe – Hollywood – has been accused of the crime almost from the day her death was announced. The men in the big executive chairs, however, treated her no better and no worse than they did any other Hollywood star of the time, most of whom have managed to survive their treatment in reasonably good shape.

Carefree Marilyn leaps along the beach at Amagansett, Long Island, where she and Arthur Miller had a summer house in 1958. Sam Shaw captured the moment.

Joseph Mankiewicz, was probably nearer the truth when he remarked to writer Gary Carey that Monroe's 'particular pattern of self-destruction had been completed long before she heard of Schwab's Drugstore', though even he admitted that the movies, and her sudden, staggering stardom 'did shape the finish for her and hurry it'. Add to this remark Pete Martin's that 'She was born afraid. She never got over it. In the end, fear killed her', and Arthur Miller's sad comment 'If she was simple it would have been easy to help her; she could have made it with a little luck', and we have a reasonable basis for understanding Marilyn Monroe's death.

In truth, there is no need to dream up thriller-type plots or to talk mawkish nonsense about the evils of the Hollywood star system to account for her death. There was more than enough stacked against her in August 1962 to make reaching for the bottle of pills almost a reflex action for someone for whom taking drugs had become as ordinary a part of her life as cleaning her teeth.

The failure of her third marriage was a blow to her self-confidence and her self-esteem. It left her alone in the world with no one really close to whom she could turn for advice or emotional support in time of need. It also meant that she was no longer the centre of someone else's world. Everyone seemed able to get along without her, while no one who mattered seemed to be finding her wonderful any more. It had been many years since she stopped thinking that the adulation of the masses was enough. She had learned that the love of millions of people who don't even know you counts for little: a couple of bad films, a few more inevitable wrinkles, and your image has lost its appeal. The masses could even begin to dislike you.

She must have known that her days as a beautiful sex goddess were coming to an end. Just two months before her death she had done two very long photographic sessions, one of them nude, for Bert Stern of *Vogue*, who was reckoned to be one of the world's leading photographers. Monroe had always been very jealous of the image her photographs presented to the world, and closely controlled the quality of what was published about her. Many of Stern's negatives and contact prints were returned to him scored through by her with the marks of a red pencil or a hair pin.

If she could have accepted the inevitable end of Monroe the sex goddess, she would still have found it hard to have had any confidence in the future of Monroe the great actress. Even in her last film, *The Misfits*, she was still getting reviews which said, in essence, 'Monroe was great. We still don't know if she was acting or just being Monroe, but it does not matter'. To her, it did matter. It mattered, too, that she had never even been nominated for an Academy Award, a nomination that would have come from the members of the Motion Picture Academy of Arts and Sciences, most of whom were her peers, people of her world.

All in all, it seems unnecessary to add sensational theories to the fact of Marilyn Monroe's death. In a sense, they diminish her, making her a pawn in someone else's game rather than the arbiter, however off-balance, of her own destiny.

It is a destiny that has been discussed and written about in dozens of books, hundreds of articles, millions of words both before and after her death, and the stream shows no sign of drying up, largely, of course, because the interest in Marilyn Monroe does not dry up, either. She has become almost an icon of our age, and reading and writing about her is one way of trying to come close to her.

Late in 1982, Joe DiMaggio cancelled an order he had first made twenty years before for roses to be placed always in front of Marilyn Monroe's tomb in a Los Angeles cemetery. He gave no reason for his action; perhaps he was trying to say that she had been dead long enough to be granted the dignity of being quietly forgotten. If so, he was fighting hopelessly against a floodtide.

Dead, Marilyn Monroe is as big business as she was alive. Perhaps even bigger, for there seems to be no limit to how she can be marketed, especially now that a Los Angeles lawyer-agent, Roger Richman, who also handles the merchandising of Elvis Presley memorabilia, has won the right to represent the Monroe estate as its sole licensing agent.

Some good may come of all this, however, since the beneficiaries of Marilyn Monroe's will – besides her half-sister

Berneice and her mother, Gladys, still alive and living in a sheltered house for the elderly – include a Child Therapy Clinic founded by Dr. Anna Freud in Hampstead, London. Marilyn left a large part of her estate to her New York psychiatrist, Dr. Maryanne Kris, who willed it in turn to Dr. Freud. The clinic is likely to benefit in the immediate future from the sale of vinyl Marilyn Monroe dolls, launched in America early in 1983 and expected to sell all over the world; presumably there will be more, much more, to come. The clinic, Berneice and Gladys may all end up richer than Marilyn herself. Not that Gladys will care. The last time a reporter asked her about her famous daughter and her career, Gladys replied, 'I am not interested in material things, I am interested only in God'.

Confident study of a mature woman: one of the many photographs taken by Vogue *photographer Bert Stern during his last photo sessions with Marilyn in 1962.*

Made for the fans: an autographed photograph of Hollywood's love goddess supreme.

Bibliography

Conversations With Marilyn, William J. Weatherby. Robson Books, London 1976.
Marilyn, Norman Mailer. Hodder and Stoughton 1973.
Marilyn – A Very Personal Story, Norman Rosten. Millington, London 1974.
Marilyn Monroe, Pete Martin. Frederick Muller 1956.
Marilyn Monroe, Maurice Zolotow. W. H. Allen 1961. Harcourt, Brace, New York 1960.

More About All About Eve, Gary Carey. Random House, New York 1972.
Norma Jean, Fred Lawrence Guiles. W. H. Allen 1969.
The Films of Marilyn Monroe, Michael Conway and Mark Ricci (Eds). Citadel, New York 1964.
The Last Sitting, Bert Stern. Orbis Publishing 1982.
Who Killed Marilyn? (And Did the Kennedy's Know?), Tony Sciacca. Manor Books 1976.

Filmography

Dangerous Years. 1947. Twentieth Century-Fox. Director: Arthur Pierson. Producer: Sol Wurtzel. Screenplay and story: Arnold Belgard. With William Halop, Anne Todd, Scotty Beckett, Jerome Cowan. Running time: 1 hour 3 mins.

Scudda Hoo! Scudda Hay! (Later changed to *Summer Lightning*). 1948. Twentieth Century-Fox. Director: F. Hugh Herbert. Producer: Walter Morosco. Screenplay: F. Hugh Herbert (from a novel by George Agnew Chamberlain). With June Haver, Lon McCallister, Walter Brennan, Anne Revere, Natalie Wood. Running time: 1 hour 35 mins. Technicolor.

Ladies of the Chorus. 1948. Columbia. Director: Phil Karlson. Producer: Harry A. Romm. Screenplay: Harry Sauber, Joseph Carole (from a story by Harry Sauber). With Adele Jergens, Randy Brooks, Nana Bryant. Running time: 61 mins.

Love Happy. 1949. United Artists. Director: David Miller. Producer: Lester Cowan. Presented by Mary Pickford. Screenplay: Frank Tashlin, Mac Benoff (from a story by Harpo Marx). With Harpo Marx, Chico Marx, Groucho Marx, Vera-Ellen, Ilona Massey, Marion Hutton, Raymond Burr. Running time: 85 mins.

A Ticket to Tomahawk. 1950. Twentieth Century-Fox. Director: Richard Sale. Producer: Robert Bassler. Written by Mary Loos and Richard Sale. With Dan Dailey, Anne Baxter, Rory Calhoun, Walter Brennan, Charles Kemper, Connie Gilchrist, Arthur Hunnicutt. Running time: 1 hour 31 mins. Technicolor.

The Asphalt Jungle. 1950. Metro-Goldwyn-Mayer. Director: John Huston. Screenplay: John Huston, Ben Maddow (from a novel by W.R. Burnett). With Sterling Hayden, Louis Calhern, Jean Hagen, James Whitmore, Sam Jaffe. Running time: 1 hour 52 min.

The Fireball. 1950. Twentieth Century-Fox. Director: Tay Garnett. Producer: Bert Friedlob. Screenplay: Tay Garnett, Horace McCoy. With Mickey Rooney, Pat O'Brien, Beverly Tyler. Running time: 1 hour 24 mins.

All About Eve. 1950. Twentieth Century-Fox. Director: Joseph L. Mankiewicz. Screenplay: Joseph L. Mankiewicz (based on the story 'The Wisdom of Eve' by Mary Orr). With Bette Davis, Anne Baxter, George Sanders, Celeste Holm, Gary Merrill, Hugh Marlowe, Thelma Ritter, Gregory Ratoff. Running time: 2 hours 8 mins.

Right Cross. 1950. Metro-Goldwyn-Mayer. Director: John Sturges. Script: Charles Schnee. With June Allyson, Dick Powell, Ricardo Montalban, Lionel Barrymore. Running time: 1 hour 29 mins.

Home Town Story. 1951. Metro-Goldwyn-Mayer. Director: Arthur Pierson. Screenplay and story: Arthur Pierson. With Jeffrey Lynn, Donald Crisp, Marjorie Reynolds. Running time: 1 hour 1 min.

As Young as You Feel. 1951. Twentieth Century-Fox. Director: Harmon Jones. Producer Lamar Trotti. Screenplay: Lamar Trotti (based on a story by Paddy Chayefsky). With Monty Woolley, Thelma Ritter, David Wayne, Jean Peters, Constance Bennett. Running time: 1 hour 17 mins.

Love Nest. 1951. Twentieth Century-Fox. Director: Joseph Newman. Producer: Jules Buck. Screenplay: I.A.L. Diamond (based on a novel by Scott Corbett). With June Haver, William Lundigan, Frank Fay, Jack Paar, Leatrice Joy. Running time: 1 hour 24 mins.

Let's Make It Legal. 1951. Twentieth Century-Fox. Director: Richard Sale. Producer: Robert Bassler. Screenplay: F. Hugh Herbert, I.A.L. Diamond (based on a story by Mortimer Braus). With Claudette Colbert, Macdonald Carey, Zachary Scott, Barbara Bates, Robert Wagner, Frank Cady. Running time: 1 hour 17 mins.

Clash by Night. 1952. R.K.O. Radio-Jerry Wald and Norman Krasna Productions. Director: Fritz Lang. Screenplay: Alfred Hayes (from a play by Clifford Odets). With Barbara Stanwyck, Paul Douglas, Robert Ryan. Running time: 1 hour 45 mins.

We're Not Married. 1952. Twentieth Century-Fox. Director: Edmund Goulding. Producer: Nunnally Johnson. Screenplay: Nunnally Johnson (adapted by Dwight Taylor from a story by Gina Kaus, Jay Dratler). With Ginger Rogers, Fred Allen, Victor Moore, David Wayne, Eve Arden, Paul Douglas, Eddie Bracken, Mitzi Gaynor, Louis Calhern, Zsa Zsa Gabor, James Gleason. Running time: 1 hour 26 mins.

Don't Bother to Knock. 1952. Twentieth Century-Fox. Director: Roy Baker. Producer: Julian Blaustein. Screenplay: Daniel Taradash (based on a novel by Charlotte Armstrong). With Richard Widmark, Anne Bancroft, Donna Corcoran. Running time: 1 hour 16 mins.

Monkey Business. 1952. Twentieth Century-Fox. Director: Howard Hawks. Screenplay: Ben Hecht, Charles Lederer, I.A.L. Diamond (from a story by Harry Segall). With Cary Grant, Ginger Rogers, Charles Coburn. Running time: 1 hour 37 mins.

O. Henry's Full House. 1952. Twentieth Century-Fox. Five short stories narrated by John Steinbeck. Marilyn Monroe appeared in the first of these, 'The Cop and the Anthem'. Director: Henry Koster. Screenplay: Lamar Trotti. With Charles Laughton,

David Wayne. Running time: 19 mins. Titles of the other episodes: 'The Clarion Call' (Director: Henry Hathaway); 'The Last Leaf' (Director: Jean Negulesco); 'The Ransom of the Red Chief' (Director: Howard Hawks); 'The Gift of the Magi' (Director: Henry King).

Niagara. 1953. Twentieth Century-Fox. Director: Henry Hathaway. Producer: Charles Brackett. Screenplay: Charles Brackett, Walter Reisch and Richard Breen. With Joseph Cotten, Jean Peters, Casey Adams. Running time: 1 hour 29 mins. Technicolor.

Gentlemen Prefer Blondes. 1953. Twentieth Century-Fox. Director: Howard Hawks. Producer: Sol C. Siegel. Screenplay: Charles Lederer (based on the musical comedy by Joseph Fields and Anita Loos). Music and lyrics: Jule Styne and Leo Robin (music and lyrics for 'When Love Goes Wrong', 'Anyone Here For Love', by Hoagy Carmichael and Harold Adamson). With Jane Russell, Charles Coburn. Running time: 1 hour 25 mins. Technicolor.

How to Marry a Millionaire. 1953. Twentieth Century-Fox. Director: Jean Negulesco. Producer: Nunnally Johnson. Screenplay: Nunnally Johnson (based on plays by Zoe Atkins 'The Greeks Had a Word For It'; Dale Eunsor and Katherine Albert 'Loco'). With Betty Grable, Lauren Bacall, David Wayne, Rory Calhoun, Cameron Mitchell, Alex D'Arcy, Fred Clark, William Powell. Running time: 1 hour 35 mins. Technicolor.

River of No Return. 1954. Twentieth Century-Fox. Director: Otto Preminger. Producer: Stanley Rubin. Screenplay: Frank Fenton (from a story by Louis Lantz). Music and lyrics for 'River of No Return', 'I'm Gonna File My Claim', 'One Silver Dollar', 'Down in the Meadow' by Lionel Newman and Ken Darby. With Robert Mitchum, Rory Calhoun, Tommy Rettig. Running time: 1 hour 31 mins. Technicolor.

There's No Business Like Show Business. 1954. Twentieth Century-Fox. Director: Walter Lang. Screenplay: Henry and Phoebe Ephron (from a story by Lamar Trotti). Music: Lionel Newman and Ken Darby. Songs: Irving Berlin. With Ethel Merman, Donald O'Connor, Dan Dailey, Johnny Ray, Mitzi Gaynor. Running time: 1 hour 57 mins. Colour by De Luxe.

The Seven Year Itch. 1955. Twentieth Century-Fox. Director: Billy Wilder. Screenplay: George Axelrod, Billy Wilder (from the stage play by George Axelrod). With Tom Ewell, Evelyn Keyes, Sonny Tufts. Running time: 1 hour 45 mins. Colour by De Luxe.

Bus Stop. 1956. Twentieth Century-Fox. Director: Joshua Logan. Screenplay: George Axelrod (based on the play by William Inge). With Don Murray, Arthur O'Connell, Betty Field. Running time: 1 hour 34 mins. Colour by De Luxe.

The Prince and the Showgirl. 1957. Warner Brothers – Marilyn Monroe Productions. Producer-Director: Laurence Olivier. Author-Scriptwriter: Terence Rattigan. Music: Richard Addinsell. With Laurence Olivier, Sybil Thorndyke, Richard Wattis, Jeremy Spenser, Esmond Knight. Running time: 1 hour 57 mins. Technicolor.

Some Like It Hot. 1959. United Artists. Producer-Director: Billy Wilder. Screenplay: Billy Wilder, I.A.L. Diamond (from a story by R. Thoxeren, M. Logan). Songs include: 'Running Wild' by Joe Gray and Leo Worth, 'I Wanna Be Loved By You' by Bert Calmar, Harry Ruby and Herbert Stothart, and 'I'm Through With Love' by Gus Kahn, Matty Malneck and F. Livingston. With Tony Curtis, Jack Lemmon, George Raft, Pat O'Brien, Joe E. Brown, Edward G. Robinson Jr. Running time: 2 hours 1 min.

Let's Make Love. 1960. Twentieth Century-Fox. Director: George Cukor. Producer: Jerry Wald. Screenplay: Norman Krasna (with additional material by Hal Kanter). Music: Lionel Newman. Words and music: Sammy Cahn, James Van Heusen. Song 'My Heart Belongs to Daddy' by Cole Porter. With Yves Montand, Frankie Vaughan, Tony Randall, Wilfred Hyde White, Running time: 1 hour 58 mins. Colour by De Luxe.

The Misfits. 1961. United Artists. Director: John Huston. Producer: Frank E. Taylor. Screenplay: Arthur Miller. With Clark Gable, Montgomery Clift, Thelma Ritter, Eli Wallach. Running time: 2 hours 4 mins.

Something's Got to Give. 1962. Twentieth Century-Fox. Director George Cukor. Screenplay: Walter Bernstein. With Dean Martin, Cyd Charisse, Phil Silvers, Wally Cox.
This film was never completed. It was re-shot with Doris Day, James Garner and Polly Bergen in the roles originally intended for Monroe, Martin and Charisse in what was a remake of *My Favourite Wife*, and called *Move Over Darling* (1963).

Index